SLOSHIES

SLOSHIES

102 BOOZY COCKTAILS STRAIGHT FROM THE FREEZER

JERRY NEVINS OF SNOW & CO.

WORKMAN PUBLISHING · NEW YORK

Library of Congress Cataloging-in-Publication Data is available.

ISBN 978-0-7611-8946-6

Design by Janet Vicario
Prop stylist: Sara Abalan
Cocktail stylist: Kate Schmidt
Illustrations by Edward McGowan

Workman books are available at special discounts when purchased in bulk for premiums
and sales promotions as well as for fund-raising or educational use. Special editions or
book excerpts can also be created to specification. For details, contact the Special Sales
Director at the address below, or send an email to specialmarkets@workman.com.

Workman Publishing Co., Inc.
225 Varick Street
New York, NY 10014-4381
workman.com

WORKMAN is a registered trademark of Workman Publishing Co., Inc.

Printed in China

First printing May 2017
10 9 8 7 6 5 4 3 2 1

THANK-YOUS

There are many amazing people who allowed this book to happen, so it's only fitting to thank them first thing. Please indulge me a moment.

To my loving wife, Robynn, and our two amazing children, Sawyer and Scarlett. Thanks for letting Daddy put giant frozen drink machines in the kitchen for months on end, giving me time to write and drink while you made sure everything ran as it should over these many years. I love you, and couldn't have written this book without your love and support. To my family, Stan, Paul, and Nancy, thanks for the support over the years to get me here.

To my business partners, Andy Talbert and Lauren Cloud, entrepreneurship is a team sport and I'm honored to be on your team. The great thing about working with people who are better than you is that you get to learn something new. I truly learn something from you every time we talk.

To Jason Burton at The Lab, we've come a long way since I randomly called you up after seeing your name in an article. Thanks for all of your patience and for teaching me the ropes as I came to you with this crazy idea of craft frozen cocktails in 2010.

To my amazing staff (past and present) who have kept things chugging along while I've been buried in my laptop writing all of this. And a special shout-out to Eric Shoemaker, Rachael Chesney, and Courtney Hollenbeck for the all-nighter giving these recipes one last makeover.

There are friends too many to name who helped in ways large and small. As they say, it takes a village to make frozen cocktails, or something like that.

CONTENTS

THE
FIRST
SNOWFALL

For thousands of years, humankind has been experimenting with fermentation. While the discovery of alcohol is somewhat shrouded in mystery because of the passage of time, it's very possible that some scrappy early farmer once experienced a light-bulb moment of discovery during a bite of fermented fruit, realizing its pleasantly buzzy properties and opening the door to experimentation with various fruits and grains.

We like to think the frozen drink was invented shortly thereafter, when our enterprising ancestors, thrilled with and possibly altered by their new invention, left their booze outside in the cold overnight and woke up to find a sloshie delight the next morning. Of course, we're completely making up this tale of accidental genius, but what's true is that ice and alcohol have been around for a long time.

However, despite this long period that could have been devoted to perfecting an artful combination of ice and alcohol, our common understanding has lately been colored by the "daiquiri bar" style of blender drink—available poolside, on a cruise ship, or (more accessibly) on the menus of some of your favorite chain restaurants. Before you roll your eyes at our snobbish ways and snap this book shut, please just know that we have had our fair share—you might say *a lot*—of those types of frozen cocktails in our lifetimes. As a matter of fact, now that we make our living on sloshies at Snow & Co., we can actually write them off as a research and development expense. (A great side benefit of owning a bar, in case you're interested.)

And while the resurgence of cocktail culture is evident across the country, the frozen cocktail has not kept pace. If you're a patron of daiquiri bars or a blender drink enthusiast, you're consuming drinks made with 151-proof, or grain, alcohol plus a bright, unnaturally colored syrup or a jug of branded pre-mix. A few notable bars are starting to bring their love of frozen cocktails out of the closet (The Tippler and Mother's Ruin in New York City and Drumbar in Chicago come to mind), with a focus and care similar to that seen in the craft cocktail scene. At Snow & Co., we didn't want to trot out just one or two amazing frozen drinks. We wanted to start a revolution of frozen cocktails—so they can hold their own next to some of the classics in the world of mixology.

Although Snow & Co. is off to an auspicious start, we have quite the hill to climb and this book is our clarion call. Our hope is that our sisters and brothers of the cocktail world take this book as an entry point and a provocation to make frozen cocktails as amazing as anything else inside their bars. After all, an awesome frozen cocktail is one of the cornerstones of any gathering of friends.

THREE MBA GRADS WALK INTO A BAR

Cocktails are collaborations between ingredients, just like businesses are collaborations between creators. The three original founders of Snow & Co.—Andy Talbert, Lauren Cloud, and Jerry Nevins (that's me)—met in grad school at the University of Missouri, Kansas City. We worked well together and knew if there was anyone we wanted to start a business with, it was each other. The only problem was that we didn't have an idea for a

The original Snow & Co. in the Crossroads Arts District of Kansas City, opened on November 4, 2011.

business. So, after we graduated, we'd kick around every Wednesday night and bring our crazy ideas to the table. Some of them were horrible, like the floating birthday candle that would sit on top of your celebratory birthday beer (feel free to steal that one). Some of them were amazing, but impossible to execute at the time, like our local version of the RED campaign that would promote local causes through sponsorship dollars and rebuild the city core of KC. Then one day in May 2010, as we talked about what we'd been up to, something unexpected happened. Not just one of us, but all three of us had spoken to completely unrelated sets of friends who lamented the lack of a good frozen cocktail in Kansas City. That's when it hit us. The idea for Snow & Co. was born.

We started out with one location, then grew to a second a few years later, both in Kansas City. (Most of you might have a general idea of where that is. If not, imagine a map of the United States. Now think of a spot smack dab in the middle of the map. There we are, on the Missouri side of the Kansas-Missouri border.) You might think it an unlikely place to start a business specializing in frozen things, if you're familiar with our Midwest winters. But despite the challenging weather during the colder months, we still couldn't let go of the fact that the people of Kansas City WANTED a frozen cocktail bar to call home. Plus, our summers can be just as hot as our winters can be bitterly cold.

As we did our homework (yes, it's a tough job, but someone has to do it), we realized that within the entire country,

BRAIN FREEZE FIRST AID

When you drink something cold quickly, the blood vessels in your upper palate constrict, sending a pain signal to the surrounding nerves. The quickest way to avoid the headache? Drink slower.

But that's easier said than done (and much less fun). Here are a couple of common remedies:

- Press your tongue against the roof of your mouth. The pressure will warm your palate back up and restore blood flow.

- Tilt your head back for about 20 seconds to increase blood flow to your palate.

we couldn't find a bar that focused on carefully crafted frozen cocktails. A handful of places were playing with the idea as part of a larger menu, but we thought it deserved to be the star of the show—a fresh, artisanal lineup featuring frozen drinks as the main event.

There were two major roadblocks to this idea, as we quickly found out.

First and foremost, people had a hard time thinking of frozen cocktails as anything other than high-octane swill. One place where we did "research" told us all the drinks were made with grain alcohol; the only difference among drinks was the syrup they added for flavor. So this led us to believe that many of the frozen drinks out there are purchased for effect, not for taste. When it came to being frozen fanatics, we had our work cut out for us in terms of changing the perception of the drinking public.

Second, from an ops perspective, most bartenders hate (and we mean capital-H *Hate*) making frozen drinks. They slow the bar service down. Bartenders would rather make ten vodka and Red Bulls, with the accompanying tip on each, than spend the same amount of time whirring together one mudslide. Bars that try to solve this problem stock their slush in large machines that freeze booze-tails in large batches. (Think of the big metal behemoths that you might find in New Orleans.) Because the demand can vary by day, week, or month, these big-batch concoctions contain shelf-stable syrups, so they can stay in the machines for a long time with no ill effects.

We felt that with the craft cocktail movement—and its emphasis on fresh, local ingredients—in full swing, we needed to follow that wave in the frozen world. So we set out on a different path—working on some recipes at home in a tiny gelato machine with fresh-squeezed juices, handmade syrups, and premium spirits, making them week after week. There were very few road maps for the granita-style cocktail, so we started with the idea that classic bar offerings could be frozen if we made the right adjustments.

Frozen cocktails are a bit different from standard cocktails, in that you not only need to work on the balance of the spirits and other ingredients, but you also need to execute the balance in a way that will allow the mixture to freeze correctly with common equipment (versus using liquid nitrogen, which can be a bear to deal with and dangerous if used incorrectly). Additionally, the temperature of the frozen cocktail will make it taste different from the same cocktail at room-temperature. Flavors aren't as sweet when frozen; aromatics get dialed down and the temperature generally acts as a mute. This has to do with the cooling of the tongue itself, which, due to the abundant vascularization of that organ, is typically hard to achieve. But frozen cocktails do the trick quite nicely.

This is a plus in our book. While cooling down your tongue pulls some flavors out of the profile initially (specifically sweet and bitter tastes), the experience of melting ice makes for a great magic trick. As you sip your drink and leave it on your tongue to warm up, those flavors and aromatics come back. It can give you a wonderfully transcendent experience of having new flavors wash upon you as the drink moves from frozen to cold to warm on the palate. (We joke it's like a drink version of the three-course-dinner chewing gum from *Charlie and the Chocolate Factory*.)

Even spice is muted by the frozen cocktail, such as in our frozen bloody Mary (Proud Mary, page 111). Capsaicin, a chemical compound that makes chile peppers hot, binds to a receptor on the tongue that senses pain, signaling to the body that the pepper's temperature is above 107°F (even though it's not—peppers are safe to eat!). Although alcohol may lower this temperature threshold, when you freeze the spicy cocktail, you are essentially offering a cold salve in tandem with the spice. If you've ever chugged a cold beer to take the sting out of hot salsa, you know what we mean. All this is to say: Dialing the temperature of your cocktail below thirty-two degrees brings out another dimension to the common drinking experience.

HEMINGWAY AND THE CROSSROADS ARTS DISTRICT

As many entrepreneurs are likely to do, we drew our fair share of naysayers as we prepared to launch our new bar. Luckily, along the way we found a creative local collaborator in Jason Burton of The LAB, a beverage consultancy based in Kansas City. And in November 2011, we opened the doors to Snow & Co., serving drinks like the Manhattan (The Rockefeller, page 101) and a wheat shandy (Sunshine Boulevard, page 38), along with many other unique delights.

To come up with the name Snow & Co., we drew inspiration from our hometown, Kansas City, and the specific history of the Crossroads Arts District, where the original Snow & Co. is located. Crossroads is a collection of century-old buildings haphazardly scattered through a neighborhood due south of the central business district of Kansas City. Alleys and intersections crisscross through a patchwork of eclectic shops, studios, galleries, and restaurants. Our section is one of a few of the nation's remaining Film Row districts, where the major studios stored and shipped all their film reels in their heyday. In addition to its charming layout, Crossroads has a literary claim to fame: It's the neighborhood that Ernest Hemingway frequented as a young reporter, perhaps enticing officers at the Crossroads police station with whiskey so he could get first crack at breaking the neighborhood's crime stories.

Hemingway is also an inspiration. He's a paradoxical character: A quintessential manly American writer known for his short prose style, Hemingway also loved frozen daiquiris (which he discovered in Cuba) filled with fresh fruit and esoteric liquors. Although he obviously went on to write works of literary greatness in other cities, we loved the image of him honing his reportage (and possibly enjoying his cocktails) in our neighborhood. He was young, but in a town run by Tom Pendergast, drinking came easily if you knew the right people. One of our favorite short stories of his is "The Snows of Kilimanjaro," so *snow* is what we decided to call our cocktails. To round out the name, we looked to Shakespeare and Company, the bookstore where so many expat writers hung out in Paris, back in the day. And so we arrived at Snow & Co.

OUR PHILOSNOWPHY

Our style of cocktails follows three simple principles. Here are the "Three Fs" of Snow & Co:

- **FUN TO DRINK:** Let's face it, some people can get a bit hoity-toity when it comes to drinking. Our dear friend Jeremy Danner, beer ambassador for Kansas City's Boulevard Brewing Company, says, "Hey, don't take this so seriously! Drinking should be fun." We wholeheartedly agree with him, so we strive to strike a balance between using fresh, premium ingredients and a technique that doesn't feel like you need a science degree or years of mixology classes to master.

- **FROZEN IN SMALL BATCHES:** With a name like Snow, it goes without saying that our style is frozen. More specifically, granita-style frozen cocktails in small batches. This strategy allows us to be speedy but also keeps the result fresh. It is our humble opinion that blenders tend to separate out the ice from the booze. Freezing all of the ingredients together in a 40 oz. batch gives you a great texture and means that every sip turns out the same.

- **FRESH FRUITS:** We believe fresh ingredients make the very best frozen cocktails. Trust us, we wish we felt differently about this; juicing thousands of citrus fruits by hand is not nearly as fast as popping them into a fancy machine. Even pre-bottled juices tend to have been processed in ways that take that special pop out of the drinks. We don't skimp here, and we suggest you not do so either.

PREPARING FOR YOUR FIRST SNOW (AKA GETTING STARTED)

The basic mechanics of the Snow & Co. cocktail are pretty simple (get things really cold), but there are a couple of best practices that we can share.

MACHINERY, OR LACK THEREOF

You don't need to get fancy to enjoy homemade frozen cocktails. There are pieces of equipment that make it easier and faster, but the basic concept of our granita-style frozen cocktails allows for flexibility—all you need is a really cold place and an airtight container to store the ingredients in.

Super Simple: A freezer bag and a freezer

Yep, that's it! A zip-top bag fulfills the airtight container requirement nicely, with little fuss. Take a freezer bag, pour the cocktail ingredients in, seal it well, and stuff that sucker in the freezer.

As it freezes, give it a gentle shake so the booze doesn't separate, and then pull it out after about 4 hours (depending on how good your freezer is and the volume of the cocktail you're freezing), and massage the bag to break up the cocktail. If you need a little assistance, run the bag quickly under some hot water and massage some more.

A freezer sloshie isn't going to have the smooth texture of gelato or a drink prepared with a professional granita machine (the ice crystals will be larger), but it won't break the bank.

Simple and Fast: A gelato or ice cream machine with an internal compressor

If you're making four or five cocktails at a time (about 40 ounces of sloshie, which is our standard recipe size in the book), you can get a good gelato or ice cream machine for two hundred to four hundred dollars and crank out these small batches in 30 to 60 minutes. Again, the time it takes to freeze depends on the volume you put in. Here's how it works: The machine freezes the metal bowl, and the cocktail mixture

then freezes to the sides of the bowl. A blade inside turns and scrapes a thin layer of the frozen cocktail off the sides and stirs it up until the entire drink is frozen.

This method will give you a velvety smooth freeze, with smaller crystals than those that form in the freezer bag method, creating a more drinkable frozen cocktail.

Give yourself at least 60 minutes to freeze a full recipe in this book. You can precool some models, which shaves off time after you put your cocktail mixture in. Breville and De'Longhi both have solid gelato machines that we've used for these purposes and we would highly recommend them. There are other brands (which will remain nameless) that caused us to curse mightily and throw things in the bar. Come to Kansas City and buy us a drink if you want those names.

A word of caution: You may think you can grab a cheaper gelato or ice cream machine that uses a pre-chilled insert. There are even some cups that claim to freeze your drinks into a slush within minutes using this pre-chilled method. If you're making one of our nonalcoholic recipes, you'll be fine with those. However, in our experience, when freezing alcoholic cocktails, those pre-chilled inserts tend not to work because alcohol lowers the freezing temperature of the liquid beyond what those units can handle. A machine with an internal compressor provides constant cooling power, which is what you need for a great sloshie. Get the machine with the internal compressor and you'll be a happy frozen-cocktail-drinking fool all of your days.

Frozen Fanatic Style: A commercial-grade granita machine

If you're having a huge party, or thinking of starting your own frozen cocktail bar, this is the option for you. Commercial granita machines start around a gallon in size and only get exponentially bigger from there. You can find companies that rent them, if you just need one for a single event. Rental companies can be a bit picky about what you put in their machines, so make sure you check with them before renting. We can assure you that our Bunn Ultra 2 machines handle the job just fine, if you wanted to pick up your own for the basement bar.

What Do We Recommend for You at Home?

We'd suggest the freezer bag method, aka the Super Simple option (page 10), as you start, and you can work your way up to the Simple and Fast option (page 11), the ice cream machine, which speeds up your freezing time and will allow you to experiment more quickly on your own. Once you graduate to the Simple and Fast ice cream machine, you can whip up multiple small batches and start a mini Snow & Co. out of your kitchen during the spring and summer months.

OTHER EQUIPMENT

What else do you need to achieve maximum sloshie? Not much! You may have these tools in your kitchen already; if not, they shouldn't set you back too much.

JIGGERS OR LIQUID MEASURING CUPS: You'll be measuring out the liquors, juices, and syrups with these. (A standard jigger is 1½ ounces.)

JUICER: You can go as simple as a handheld citrus press, or move up to a tabletop press or an electric juicer. Either way, a tool to get the most out of your citrus fruit will be essential.

STRAINER: A simple fine-mesh strainer will allow you to remove any unwanted pulp and seeds from your juices, as well as to remove herbs and such from your infusions.

IMMERSION BLENDER: When making drinks with milk as a base, the immersion blender helps you quickly emulsify the cocktail so the milk won't separate and curdle as the cocktail freezes together. Don't skimp on this piece or think you can just whisk it. A regular blender will work to create emulsions, too: Just pour the cream ingredients in slowly after you've combined everything else.

INFUSION JARS/CONTAINERS: When you make the infused syrups and alcohols on pages 17–22, you'll need to store them in simple airtight containers. No fancy rules here—you can pick your aesthetic, so that can be a canning jar, hermetic clamp seal, screw-on, and so forth.

GLASSWARE

As we researched glassware at our inception, we quickly learned we had much in common with the coffee industry. We both needed to keep a product at a temperature much different from room temperature for long periods of time. We also needed to keep our guests from feeling the effects on their hands. (And we'd prefer not to harm the planet in the process—meaning plastic and Styrofoam were out.) While many companies have built great glassware geared toward temperature retention, we fell in love with Bodum double-walled glassware. No more napkins wrapped around tiki mugs or daiquiri glasses. No ill effects on the environment. Additionally, these glasses act as their own sort of flair for our style of drink. They may not be traditional, but we think they are an innovation in how frozen cocktails should be served.

Of course, we will not judge if we see you serving frozen drinks in something other than a double-walled glass. Again, this is about having fun—if you want to serve them in a Moscow mule mug, traditional tiki tumbler, and so on, that's cool with us, too. Don't break the bank. We just want you to know what works best to keep the drinks frozen and your fingers room temperature.

FLARED (PINT)

The perfect all-purpose frozen cocktail glass (and also what we use at Snow & Co.). A solid choice, this glass can pull off any cocktail in the book.

RIPPLED (HIGHBALL OR DECORATIVE)

If you want to pick up a great secondary glass to add some variety to your frozen drink presentation, this one can also be a workhorse as you prepare most of the drinks in this book.

UP & DOWN (OLD FASHIONED OR ROCKS)

This small but stately glass makes for a great effect when serving whiskey- or bourbon-based drinks.

ROUND & ROUND (CORDIAL OR SNIFTER)

A beautifully rounded glass that can be used for a simple but elegant presentation.

WENDY WINER (WINEGLASS)

A stemless wine glass will do just as well here. This vessel will work best for your frozen wine-based cocktails at special events.

FLORAL BOWL (COUPE)

Because frozen cocktails bring the aromatics down in the drink, use a wide-mouth vessel to allow the nose to grab the full floral scent from frozen cocktails.

BUBBLES BUBBLES (FLUTE)

While the bubbles have already escaped from your frozen sparkling wine, a fluted style reminds your guests they're drinking bubbly in a lower-temperature form.

PILS & CHILLS (PILSNER)

A solid choice for beer- and cider-based frozen cocktails, reminiscent of the style used to serve frosty brews.

COFFREEZE & TEAS (MUG)

Another frozen glass that can perform double duty: This one can function as a coffee or tea mug during the morning hours. Unless, of course, you're off work and starting the tippling early.

THE BUILDING BLOCKS

A house—and a sloshie—is only as good as the foundation it rests upon. Fresh juices, as we've said before, make a difference. Real homemade syrups make a difference. And oh my goodness do handmade boozy infusions make a difference. Before you start your journey down sloshie lane, get these things ready for your adventure.

FRESH JUICES

It's pretty easy to get your hands on some decent citrus and fruit juices these days. But while it may be convenient, it's definitely not the *best* way to add fruit to your drink. Juice it fresh and we promise you'll taste the difference. In a pinch, we can recommend a few replacements for things like pomegranate, cranberry, pineapple, and peach juices. But since citrus is so easy and abundant, you won't see a recommendation on a replacement for fresh-squeezed there. We promise, it's worth it!

Citrus Fruits

If you're hosting huge parties or plan to set up a serious bar in your backyard, consider investing in an electric juicer—an appliance worth its weight in gold. But for the small amounts listed in this book, a hand juicer or a citrus press will work best. A good squeeze will (roughly) yield the following quantities of juice:

LIME
1 lime = 1½ ounces of juice

LEMON
1 lemon = 2 ounces of juice

ORANGE
1 orange = 3½ ounces of juice

GRAPEFRUIT

1 grapefruit = 6 to 8 ounces of juice

Note: Size varies widely in grapefruits, so it's best to measure this one.

Other Fruits

Commercially available pineapple and cranberry juices are pretty good. While we may be more fanatical, we do realize you may not want to grab a macerating juicer just for a small amount of these juices. Go, with our blessing, and buy the commercially produced stuff. (Of course, we applaud those who take the extra step.) If you do have the equipment to turn these fruits into juice, here's what to expect:

PINEAPPLE

1 regular pineapple = 10 to 12 ounces of juice

CRANBERRY

12 ounces of cranberries = 8 ounces of juice

Note: To temper the natural cranberry flavor, you may want to drop in a bit of sugar (start with 2 or 3 tablespoons) and lemon juice, to your liking.

SYRUPS AND INFUSIONS

Frozen cocktails are easy, but a little bit of prep work is necessary to make them as tasty as can be. As with the juice ingredients, fresh is always better, and by making syrups at home, you can leave out a lot of the junk that keeps these mixers shelf-stable but impacts their taste. Plus, when you master syrups and infusions, your friends will be in awe. Only we will know the secret of how easy those two things really are.

Basic Syrups

1 Place the water and sweetener in a saucepan over medium heat and bring to a boil.

2 Reduce the heat to a simmer and stir the mixture, letting the sweetener dissolve until the liquid looks uniform, without any visible granules or streaks from the sugar, agave, or honey, about 3 minutes.

3 Remove from the heat and let the syrup cool. Use immediately or store in an airtight container in your refrigerator for up to 2 weeks.

PRO TIP:

Measure the water and sugar separately. If you put 1½ cups sugar in a three-cup container and top it off, you'll end up with a weaker syrup.

Syrup Type	Sweetener	Water	Yield
Simple Syrup	1½ cups pure cane sugar	1½ cups boiling water	2¼ cups (18 ounces) simple syrup
Agave Syrup	1½ cups agave nectar	1½ cups boiling water	3 cups (24 ounces) agave simple syrup
Honey Syrup	2 cups honey	1 cup boiling water	3 cups (24 ounces) honey simple syrup

Infused Syrups

Punch up the flavor for your syrups by infusing them with other ingredients. Nothing beats the look on someone's face when you say you made your own tarragon-infused simple syrup.

1 Place simple syrup in a saucepan over medium heat.

2 Add the ingredients from the chart below and heat for 12 minutes. Taste it after the 12 minutes have elapsed; if you can taste the flavor, it's good to go. If for some reason your strawberry syrup doesn't taste much like strawberries, leave it on a bit longer.

3 Strain out the infusion ingredients with a fine-mesh strainer, then let the syrup cool. Place it in a sealed container, and store it in the refrigerator for up to 1 week.

Note: If you want to use fresh herbs instead of dried, just triple the dried herb measurement and cut the heating time in half. Dried herbs have more concentrated flavors than fresh, but it takes a little longer to bring them out.

For 16 oz. of Simple Syrup:

Infused Syrup Flavor	Infusion Ingredient
Strawberry Simple Syrup	6 strawberries, stems removed, muddled into the syrup
Mint Simple Syrup	5 tablespoons dried mint
Lavender Simple Syrup	3 tablespoons culinary-grade lavender
Rosemary Simple Syrup	3 tablespoons dried rosemary
Tarragon Simple Syrup	3 tablespoons dried French tarragon
Cinnamon Simple Syrup	1 cinnamon stick

Infused Liquors

Even easier than infusing simple syrups is infusing alcohol with other flavors. Vodka is the most impressionable liquor—it can stand up to a number of distinct flavors well.

CINNAMON-INFUSED TITO'S VODKA

4 sticks of cinnamon

16 ounces Tito's Handmade Vodka

① Place the cinnamon sticks and the vodka in a tightly sealed container.

② Store in a cool, dark place for at least 48 hours.

STRAWBERRY-INFUSED TITO'S VODKA

12 strawberries, stemmed and halved

16 ounces Tito's Handmade Vodka

① Place the strawberries and the vodka in a tightly sealed container.

② Store in a cool, dark place for at least 48 hours. The strawberries will lose their color, but you can remove them and add new strawberries for visual appeal, and for more flavor.

JALAPEÑO-INFUSED TITO'S VODKA

2 large jalapeños, sliced into wheels

16 ounces Tito's Handmade Vodka

① Place the sliced jalapeños and the vodka in a tightly sealed container.

② Store in a cool, dark place for at least 48 hours, then strain out the jalapeños (otherwise it can get really strong). Use the jalapeños for garnish, if desired.

GINGER-INFUSED TITO'S VODKA

1 teaspoon coarsely grated peeled fresh ginger

16 ounces Tito's Handmade Vodka

① Place the ginger and the vodka in a tightly sealed container.

② Store in a cool, dark place for at least 24 hours. Strain out the ginger before using.

HONEY-ROASTED PEANUT–INFUSED TITO'S VODKA

1 cup (8 ounces) honey-roasted peanuts

14 ounces Tito's Handmade Vodka

1 Place the peanuts and the vodka in a tightly sealed container.

2 Store in a cool, dark place for at least 24 hours. Strain out the peanuts before using.

CHERRY-INFUSED OLD OVERHOLT RYE WHISKEY

1 Place 1 dark, sweet cherry (frozen works really well) per ounce of Old Overholt Rye Whiskey in a tightly sealed container.

2 Store in a cool, dark place for at least 72 hours, then strain out the cherries to use for garnish, if desired.

BRAND-NAME LIQUORS

In this book, you'll find that we've called for specific brands in our recipes, so that you can replicate the drink exactly as we'd make it at Snow & Co. But when we call for Stellina di Notte Prosecco in our recipe, you can really use any prosecco. If you want to create the drink exactly as we'd make it in the bar, the brand name will help you get there, but if you just want to use up the Italian bubbly that you have on hand, you have our blessing.

When you're looking to substitute an ingredient—or in case your local booze vendor doesn't carry the brand we call for—look to swap in something that's of a similar caliber and flavor profile. For instance, in the case of beer, substitute an ale for an ale (a Farmhouse Ale in the case of Field of Dreams, page 85) or a fruity Gose with another floral sour brew (Gose in the Shell, page 67). Same goes for wines and sparklers.

Hard alcohols may require a bit more research—you want to add the same balance of juniper and citrus into the Gin Fo'Shizzle (page 84) as you might find in a Pinckney Bend. Liqueurs and other flavored specialties should be a little more straightforward and easier to swap in and out. But since the first rule of *Sloshies* is FUN TO DRINK (see page 90), we want to help you get a quality frozen drink in your hand without a hitch.

SPICED RED WINE INFUSION

1 cinnamon stick

8 whole cloves

4 strips orange zest

Cheesecloth with tie

1 bottle decent Cabernet Sauvignon (under $15 a bottle is fine; we use Dynamite Vineyards Cabernet Sauvignon)

① Place the cinnamon, cloves, and orange zest in the cheesecloth and tie it shut.

② Place the wine in a saucepan over high heat, and drop in the cheesecloth bundle. Bring to a boil, then reduce to a simmer and stir for 10 minutes.

③ If you are not using the infusion immediately, discard the bundle, cool the infusion, and then place in a tightly sealed container. Store in the refrigerator for up to 2 days.

CHAMOMILE-INFUSED GIN

1 tea bag of Stash Organic Chamomile Herbal Tea

16 ounces Pinckney Bend Gin (Beefeater also works)

① Place the tea bag and the gin in a tightly sealed container.

② Store in a cool, dark place for 48 hours, then remove the tea bag.

COFFEE BEAN–INFUSED BULLEIT BOURBON WHISKEY

¼ cup (2 ounces) fruity whole-roasted coffee beans

16 ounces Bulleit Bourbon Frontier Whiskey

① Place the coffee beans and the bourbon in a tightly sealed container.

② Store in a cool, dark place for at least 48 hours, then strain out the beans.

Infused Fruit Skewers

As the fruit flavors and juices move out of these infusions, the spirits move into the ingredient, which means flavored booze and boozy garnish. Don't toss them—instead, skewer these high-proof pieces and place them atop your frozen concoctions.

FROZEN FLAIR

Garnishes on traditionally liquid offerings tend to be one of two extremes: super simple, or so difficult you don't even want to attempt one. A strip of orange rind in an old-fashioned or a celery stalk on your bloody Mary are nice, but expected, touches. A five-step carved pineapple may be more than you want to try.

Stencils

Because they offer a bit more texture and substance than your typical liquid beverage, frozen cocktails allow a different palette to paint upon. Much in the same way that coffee baristas create latte art when they spoon the milk and foam over the espresso, you can create effects on the top of the frozen cocktail using stencils. We like to call this "frozen flair"—it's one step beyond a garnish. You, of course, aren't required to have a certain amount of flair on your cocktail, but if you want to show off, we can help.

Select a Template

Think of those holiday sugar cookies with festive designs on top . . . except this is for your sloshie. There's no limit to what you can do, except your imagination (or internet searching capabilities). First, you'll need some simple food-grade silicone or plastic stencils. These are easy to find at craft stores or online retailers.

If you're the crafty type, you can trace and cut shapes out of a take-out container lid. Use the downloadable stencil templates at workman.com/sloshies—you'll see examples throughout the book—or create your own!

Choose Your Dust

Filling in the stencil can be as easy as selecting a cylinder of cinnamon or nutmeg from your spice rack or sifting some powdered sugar to use as dust.

If you can't find a spice that's suitable flavor-wise, and powdered sugar won't provide contrast, try adding a few drops of all-natural food coloring to a small bowl of pure cane sugar. Mix the sugar and food coloring together with a small fork or spoon to remove any lumps. Add the color a little bit at a time, stirring until you get the desired hue. Once you're happy with it, leave the sugar in an uncovered container to dry out for a few hours.

Pour, Dust, and Serve

When pouring your sloshie, leave a little room (about the width of your pinky finger) at the top of the glass. Place the stencil of your choice on top of the glass to stabilize it, then take the sugar or spice and dust it lightly over the top.

If you'd rather freehand instead of stencil, use a light syrupy drizzle or dusting of delicate flakes to coat the top of the drink. Delicious toppings can include coconut flakes, shaved chocolate, ground coffee or espresso, crushed candy, crumbled cookies or graham crackers, grated ginger, citrus zests, luster dust*, dark chocolate sauce, maple syrup, dulce de leche or caramel sauce, honey, hibiscus syrup, raspberry sauce, or butterscotch sauce.

Flower Blossoms

For some of the more floral sloshies, a blossom or sprig from the flowers in the base spirit gives you two things. First, it adds a nice visual flair and a clue to what your guests are about to imbibe. Second, because the freezing process mutes aromatics, the sprig or blossom helps add that aromatic back. We drink as much with our noses as we do with our tongues, so it's a great addition to your cocktails.

*Nontoxic, food-grade luster dust can be purchased at online retailers, craft stores like Michaels, and party or baking supply stores.

HOW TO AVALANCHE
(FEEDING FROZEN COCKTAILS TO THE MASSES)

Spreading the frozen cocktail love to all of your friends? Here are a few serving ideas, depending on the size of your crew.

AT HOME

No ordinary pitcher will do when it comes to frozen drinks! Grab some ice and **a pitcher with an insert to serve up larger batches** while keeping them cool. Fill the insert with ice water and 1 teaspoon salt to drop that temp a bit more (salt water has a lower freezing point) and keep things frosty. The insert can function as a built-in stirring stick, allowing you to keep things the right consistency without constantly running to the freezer.

OUTDOORS

Wheels are your friend when you're moving a sloshie to an outdoor location, so look for a **rolling cooler**, preferably with a luggage-style handle, to transport your precious frozen cargo. You'll need a ladle to stir and serve directly out of the top (liquid will naturally run to the bottom, so if your cooler has a spout, don't use that). It will keep your drink frozen for several hours of fun.

WHEN YOU NEED TO MAKE A TREK

Stealing again from the coffee industry, we found that **collapsible take-out coffee boxes** with an inner inflatable bag (like the ones you get with a catering order) will do the trick for transport. You can use this box and bag arrangement to freeze the sloshie, too—it will function just as well as a freezer bag. Just give it about 24 hours in the freezer. Each will hold 96 ounces.

HOW TO USE THIS BOOK

We're happy to share our recipes and approach to artful frozen cocktails with you in this book, as we believe great frozen cocktails belong to everyone, not just the lucky denizens of Kansas City.

We've organized recipes in terms of our major flavor profiles for frozen cocktails: tart, sweet, spiced, and floral. There's a cheat sheet in the back for those of you who like to pick your drinks based on primary spirit, so don't worry if you have a surplus of gin that you need help "getting rid of." For our non-drinkers, we've included a few recipes for tasty frozen mocktails, or faux-zen cocktails, if you will.

Before we get started, here are a few tips that will help you on your arctic journey.

1. Line up and mix the ingredients in the order we give you here. With the exception of milk, we've listed them from least to most expensive, which comes in handy when you, say, make the mistake of forgetting where you are in the recipe. This order allows you to start over with the least amount of financial pain.

2. Milk always goes in last and is slowly blended in with your handy dandy immersion blender. This helps emulsify the cocktail so the milk doesn't separate (and it will).

3. Speaking of the milk, use whole milk (see page 28). It's just tastier that way. The added fat also keeps the drink from separating. Trust us here, and save your calorie counting for something else.

"WHY MILK?"

We get this question a lot, and it's a fair one. There are two reasons. First, using whole milk adds fat to the drink, which in turn adds a different flavor profile. Second, adding whole milk gives the frozen cocktail a finer consistency, as the milk causes the ice granules to be smaller than in non-milk-based frozen cocktails. Smaller ice granules make for a silkier and tastier drink, in our humble opinion.

Can you sub out whole milk for a lower-fat version or for a nondairy alternative like almond or soy milk? Sure, but it's going to have an effect on the taste and on the consistency of the recipes. Less fat means the ingredients will separate more easily.

If you're going to use a low-fat product or a milk substitute, we definitely recommend you whip up your beverages with the ice cream or gelato maker, rather than using the freezer and freezer bag method. The faster freezing time and constant stirring will help combat the separation issues for you.

THE
RECIPES

TART

the red rover
(page 35)

whiskey smashed
(page 32)

peachy keen
(page 47)

nights of ni
(page 46)

WHISKEY SMASHED

Give your Kentucky Derby party an extra kick with this smashing combination of small-batch Kentucky bourbon on top of a citrus blend and minty frozen love.

ABV
9.77%

GLASS
Up & Down

GARNISH
mint leaf, lemon wheel, and a floppy hat (for you to wear)

- 2¾ ounces water
- 9 ounces Simple Syrup (page 18)
- 7¼ ounces Mint Simple Syrup (page 19)
- 6 ounces lemon juice
- 6¾ ounces lime juice
- **8¾ ounces Woodford Reserve Kentucky Straight Bourbon Whiskey**

Combine → Place the ingredients in a medium-size metal bowl and stir.

Freeze → Pour the liquid into a large freezer bag and place it in the freezer until frozen, approximately 4 hours. Alternatively, pour the liquid into an ice cream maker and proceed per the manufacturer's instructions (see page 11).

Serve → When you're ready to drink, massage the freezer bag by hand until it's a wet, slushy consistency. If it's not breaking up, run the bag quickly under hot water and massage some more.

Yield → Makes at least 4 drinks.

DOVE'S TEARS

A frozen take on the classic Paloma (meaning "dove"), this drink is not too demanding. Dig, if you will: tequila, a light wave of lime, and grapefruit. We imagine this is what it tastes like when doves cry.

ABV
7.16%

GLASS
Rippled

GARNISH
candied grapefruit peel, salted rim, and *The Very Best of Prince*

- ¾ ounce water
- 4¼ ounces Agave Syrup (page 18)
- 2¾ ounces lime juice
- 25½ ounces Izze Sparkling Grapefruit soda
- **7¼ ounces Olmeca Altos Reposado Tequila**

Combine → Place the ingredients in a medium-size metal bowl and stir.

Freeze → Pour the liquid into a large freezer bag and place it in the freezer until frozen, approximately 4 hours. Alternatively, pour the liquid into an ice cream maker and proceed per the manufacturer's instructions (see page 11).

Serve → When you're ready to drink, massage the freezer bag by hand until it's a wet, slushy consistency. If it's not breaking up, run the bag quickly under hot water and massage some more.

Yield → Makes at least 4 drinks.

CHA CHA BUCHA

Roll call! We've got kombucha, and then some citrus. It's kinda earthy, but check it out. The probiotics of the kombucha will lighten anyone's mood; they might even help those split ends. Saying it as a friend.

ABV
10.29%

GLASS
Rippled

GARNISH
gold luster-dusted lemon wheel (see page 24) and a Spartans cheerleading outfit

- 1½ ounces water
- 4½ ounces Simple Syrup (page 18)
- 4½ ounces lemon juice
- 18½ ounces GT's Kombucha Original
- **4½ ounces Caravella Limoncello Originale**
- **6¾ ounces Tito's Handmade Vodka**

Combine → Place the ingredients in a medium-size metal bowl and stir.

Freeze → Pour the liquid into a large freezer bag and place it in the freezer until frozen, approximately 4 hours. Alternatively, pour the liquid into an ice cream maker and proceed per the manufacturer's instructions (see page 11).

Serve → When you're ready to drink, massage the freezer bag by hand until it's a wet, slushy consistency. If it's not breaking up, run the bag quickly under hot water and massage some more.

Yield → Makes at least 4 drinks.

THE RED ROVER

A bit of rye mixed with some sweet vermouth and some ruby-red Cherry Heering will make just about anyone come right over . . . as long as you're willing to share.

ABV
18.27%

GLASS
Wendy Winer

GARNISH
fresh cherries on a skewer

- 7½ ounces Simple Syrup (page 18)

- 7½ ounces orange juice

- **4 ounces Cinzano Rosso Sweet Vermouth**

- **7¼ ounces Old Overholt Rye Whiskey**

- **4 ounces Cherry Heering Liqueur**

- 9¾ ounces whole milk

Combine → Place the simple syrup, orange juice, vermouth, whiskey, and cherry liqueur in a medium-size metal bowl and stir.

Blend → Add the milk to the bowl slowly, using an immersion blender to emulsify the mixture.

Freeze → Pour the liquid into a large freezer bag and place it in the freezer until frozen, approximately 4 hours. Alternatively, pour the liquid into an ice cream maker and proceed per the manufacturer's instructions (see page 11).

Serve → When you're ready to drink, massage the freezer bag by hand until it's a wet, slushy consistency. If it's not breaking up, run the bag quickly under hot water and massage some more.

Yield → Makes at least 4 drinks.

PISCO BEACH

We meant to make a left turn at Albuquerque and then maybe a right turn at La Jolla, but we found this frozen treasure instead. With a pop of pisco and applejack washing over you on waves of citrusy lemon-lime, you'll feel rich. You'll feel wealthy. Or at least comfortably well-off.

ABV
17.23%

GLASS
Flared

GARNISH
lime twist, stencil with a lattice pattern (see page 23), and the "Ali Baba Bunny" episode from *Looney Tunes*

- 5 ounces water
- 6¾ ounces Simple Syrup (page 18)
- 4¼ ounces lemon juice
- 7¼ ounces lime juice
- 8¼ ounces Laird's Applejack
- 8¼ ounces Pisco Portón

lattice stencil

Combine → Place the ingredients in a medium-size metal bowl and stir.

Freeze → Pour the liquid into a large freezer bag and place it in the freezer until frozen, approximately 4 hours. Alternatively, pour the liquid into an ice cream maker and proceed per the manufacturer's instructions (see page 11).

Serve → When you're ready to drink, massage the freezer bag by hand until it's a wet, slushy consistency. If it's not breaking up, run the bag quickly under hot water and massage some more.

Yield → Makes at least 4 drinks.

VESPER'S VARIATION

Did you know the Vesper Martini of James Bond fame was based on a frozen fruit, herb, and rum concoction in Jamaica? Neither did we, until we went to name this drink! Cheers to Wikipedia, this drink, and James Bond.

ABV
8.28%

GLASS
Round & Round

GARNISH
grapefruit wheel and *Casino Royale*

- **1 teaspoon Fee Brothers Lemon Bitters**
- 29 ounces grapefruit juice
- **5½ ounces Pisco Portón**
- **5½ ounces Cocchi Americano Aperitif Wine**

Combine → Place the ingredients in a medium-size metal bowl and stir.

Freeze → Pour the liquid into a large freezer bag and place it in the freezer until frozen, approximately 4 hours. Alternatively, pour the liquid into an ice cream maker and proceed per the manufacturer's instructions (see page 11).

Serve → When you're ready to drink, massage the freezer bag by hand until it's a wet, slushy consistency. If it's not breaking up, run the bag quickly under hot water and massage some more.

Yield → Makes at least 4 drinks.

SUNSHINE BOULEVARD

This is Snow & Co.'s original frozen shandy. The Boulevard wheat beer intensifies with the addition of vodka and fresh citrus, presenting you with California summertime in a glass.

ABV
6.52%

GLASS
Pils & Chills

GARNISH
orange sun stencil
(see page 23),
and sunshine

sun stencil

- 3 ounces water
- 8¼ ounces Simple Syrup (page 18)
- 8¼ ounces lemon juice
- 3 ounces orange juice
- **19¾ ounces Boulevard Unfiltered Wheat Beer**
- **5¾ ounces Tito's Handmade Vodka**

Combine → Place the ingredients in a medium-size metal bowl and stir.

Freeze → Pour the liquid into a large freezer bag and place it in the freezer until frozen, approximately 4 hours. Alternatively, pour the liquid into an ice cream maker and proceed per the manufacturer's instructions (see page 11).

Serve → When you're ready to drink, massage the freezer bag by hand until it's a wet, slushy consistency. If it's not breaking up, run the bag quickly under hot water and massage some more.

Yield → Makes at least 4 drinks.

BULLEIT WITH IPA WINGS

What's more refreshing than a shandy? You guessed it . . . a frozen shandy. This variation on our classic frozen shandy uses the bite of bourbon and the hoppiness of IPA to round out the citrus flavors.

ABV
6.53%

GLASS
Pils & Chills

GARNISH
beer cap glued to skewer with candied orange peel, and Smashing Pumpkins

- 1¾ ounces water

- 4¾ ounces Simple Syrup (page 18)

- 5 ounces lemon juice

- 6¾ ounces orange juice

- **18¾ ounces Boulevard Single-Wide IPA**

- **3½ ounces Bulleit Bourbon Frontier Whiskey**

Combine → Place the ingredients in a medium-size metal bowl and stir.

Freeze → Pour the liquid into a large freezer bag and place it in the freezer until frozen, approximately 4 hours. Alternatively, pour the liquid into an ice cream maker and proceed per the manufacturer's instructions (see page 11).

Serve → When you're ready to drink, massage the freezer bag by hand until it's a wet, slushy consistency. If it's not breaking up, run the bag quickly under hot water and massage some more.

Yield → Makes at least 4 drinks.

LEMON TART

Drink your dessert with a creamy and light burst of limoncello. A fresh and simple patio favorite!

ABV
8.23%

GLASS
Flared

GARNISH
candied lemon peel, silver luster dust (see page 24)

- 2¾ ounces water
- 8½ ounces Simple Syrup (page 18)
- 8½ ounces lemon juice
- **11¾ ounces Caravella Limoncello Originale**
- 8½ ounces whole milk

Combine → Place the water, simple syrup, lemon juice, and limoncello in a medium-size metal bowl and stir.

Blend → Add the milk to the bowl slowly, using an immersion blender to emulsify the mixture.

Freeze → Pour the liquid into a large freezer bag and place it in the freezer until frozen, approximately 4 hours. Alternatively, pour the liquid into an ice cream maker and proceed per the manufacturer's instructions (see page 11).

Serve → When you're ready to drink, massage the freezer bag by hand until it's a wet, slushy consistency. If it's not breaking up, run the bag quickly under hot water and massage some more.

Yield → Makes at least 4 drinks.

LIMEY BASTARD

This refresher puts the *lime* in *blimey*! Get your UK on with Hendrick's Gin, a kiss of cucumber liqueur, and fresh citrus.

ABV
6.35%

GLASS
Floral Bowl

GARNISH
green British flag stencil (see page 23) and Jason Statham

British flag stencil

- 2 ounces water
- 9½ ounces Simple Syrup (page 18)
- 3½ ounces lime juice
- 4¾ ounces lemon juice
- **8¾ ounces Thatcher's Organic Cucumber Liqueur**
- **2¾ ounces Hendrick's Gin**
- 8½ ounces whole milk

Combine → Place the water, simple syrup, lime juice, lemon juice, cucumber liqueur, and gin in a medium-size metal bowl and stir.

Blend → Add the milk to the bowl slowly, using an immersion blender to emulsify the mixture.

Freeze → Pour the liquid into a large freezer bag and place it in the freezer until frozen, approximately 4 hours. Alternatively, pour the liquid into an ice cream maker and proceed per the manufacturer's instructions (see page 11).

Serve → When you're ready to drink, massage the freezer bag by hand until it's a wet, slushy consistency. If it's not breaking up, run the bag quickly under hot water and massage some more.

Yield → Makes at least 4 drinks.

MISS SCARLETT

Frankly, my dear, you won't give a damn, either, after tasting this perfectly Southern concoction of Bulleit Bourbon, Stirrings Peach, and fresh lemon.

ABV
9.07%

GLASS
Flared

GARNISH
lemon twist, red dress stencil (see page 23), and your favorite draperies

- 3¼ ounces water
- 9¾ ounces Simple Syrup (page 18)
- 9¾ ounces lemon juice
- **7½ ounces Stirrings Peach Liqueur**
- **5 ounces Bulleit Bourbon Frontier Whiskey**
- 5 ounces whole milk

dress stencil

Combine → Place the water, simple syrup, lemon juice, peach liqueur, and whiskey in a medium-size metal bowl and stir.

Blend → Add the milk to the bowl slowly, using an immersion blender to emulsify the mixture.

Freeze → Pour the liquid into a large freezer bag and place it in the freezer until frozen, approximately 4 hours. Alternatively, pour the liquid into an ice cream maker and proceed per the manufacturer's instructions (see page 11).

Serve → When you're ready to drink, massage the freezer bag by hand until it's a wet, slushy consistency. If it's not breaking up, run the bag quickly under hot water and massage some more.

Yield → Makes at least 4 drinks.

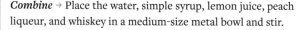

HEMINGWAY IN KC

It may be a complete fiction, but we like to imagine that Hemingway would come back to Kansas City and visit his old friends from his days of writing for the *Kansas City Star*. This silky jasmine daiquiri variation with fresh lime and Bacardi is what we'd have served him if he made a stop at Snow.

ABV
11.63%

GLASS
Floral Bowl

GARNISH
candied lime wheel, gold luster dust (see page 24), and "The Snows of Kilimanjaro"

- 5 ounces Simple Syrup (page 18)
- 7½ ounces lime juice
- 4¼ ounces grapefruit juice
- **8¼ ounces Bacardi White Rum**
- **6¾ ounces Fruit Lab Jasmine Organic Liqueur**
- 8¼ ounces whole milk

Combine → Place the simple syrup, lime juice, grapefruit juice, rum, and jasmine liqueur in a medium-size metal bowl and stir.

Blend → Add the milk to the bowl slowly, using an immersion blender to emulsify the mixture.

Freeze → Pour the liquid into a large freezer bag and place it in the freezer until frozen, approximately 4 hours. Alternatively, pour the liquid into an ice cream maker and proceed per the manufacturer's instructions (see page 11).

Serve → When you're ready to drink, massage the freezer bag by hand until it's a wet, slushy consistency. If it's not breaking up, run the bag quickly under hot water and massage some more.

Yield → Makes at least 4 drinks.

LOVELY RITA

Standing by a parking meter, when we started mixing 'ritas . . . Make sure to give the keys to the meter maid after you start in on a batch of this simple granita-style margarita. The freshly squeezed lime juice, great tequila, and orange liqueur will help this drink tow your heart away.

ABV
5.96%

GLASS
Round & Round

GARNISH
lime wheel, salted rim

- 8¾ ounces water
- 16 ounces Agave Syrup (page 18)
- 9½ ounces lime juice
- **3 ounces Olmeca Altos Reposado Tequila**
- **3 ounces Cointreau Triple Sec**

Combine → Place the ingredients in a medium-size metal bowl and stir.

Freeze → Pour the liquid into a large freezer bag and place it in the freezer until frozen, approximately 4 hours. Alternatively, pour the liquid into an ice cream maker and proceed per the manufacturer's instructions (see page 11).

Serve → When you're ready to drink, massage the freezer bag by hand until it's a wet, slushy consistency. If it's not breaking up, run the bag quickly under hot water and massage some more.

Yield → Makes at least 4 drinks.

SMOKEY AND THE BANDITO

When you're on the run, this sweet cranberry flourish with a smoky mescal finish will keep your motor running.

ABV
12.17%

GLASS
Rippled

GARNISH
fresh cranberries, and a Burt Reynolds mustache

- 23¼ ounces Lakewood Pure cranberry juice
- 5 ounces Agave Syrup (page 18)
- **8¼ ounces Del Maguey Crema de Mezcal Single Village Mezcal**
- **3¼ ounces Tanqueray No. Ten Gin**

Combine → Place the ingredients in a medium-size metal bowl and stir.

Freeze → Pour the liquid into a large freezer bag and place it in the freezer until frozen, approximately 4 hours. Alternatively, pour the liquid into an ice cream maker and proceed per the manufacturer's instructions (see page 11).

Serve → When you're ready to drink, massage the freezer bag by hand until it's a wet, slushy consistency. If it's not breaking up, run the bag quickly under hot water and massage some more.

Yield → Makes at least 4 drinks.

NIGHTS OF NI

Get puckered with a double dose of grapefruit—a fruity, fizzy soda and a ruby-red shrub—blended with finely aged Altos Reposado Tequila. "Bring us a shrubbery" will take on a whole new meaning.

ABV
9.88%

GLASS
Bubbles Bubbles

GARNISH
vodka-infused jalapeño wheel (see page 20)

- 9½ ounces water
- 5¼ ounces Agave Syrup (page 18)
- 14 ounces Izze Sparkling Grapefruit soda
- 1¾ ounces Salt & Flint Pamplemousse + Thyme Shrub Syrup
- **3½ ounces Tito's Handmade Vodka**
- **6¼ ounces Olmeca Altos Reposado Tequila**

Combine → Place the ingredients in a medium-size metal bowl and stir.

Freeze → Pour the liquid into a large freezer bag and place it in the freezer until frozen, approximately 4 hours. Alternatively, pour the liquid into an ice cream maker and proceed per the manufacturer's instructions (see page 11).

Serve → When you're ready to drink, massage the freezer bag by hand until it's a wet, slushy consistency. If it's not breaking up, run the bag quickly under hot water and massage some more.

Yield → Makes at least 4 drinks.

PEACHY KEEN

If Rizzo's mood in *Grease* were a drink, this would be it—sweet peach with a sassy juniper punch from the Hendrick's. Great for drinking at the drive-in.

ABV
10.45%

GLASS
Floral Bowl

GARNISH
gold luster-dusted peach slice (see page 24)

- 4 ounces water

- 11½ ounces Simple Syrup (page 18)

- 3 ounces lemon juice

- 11¾ ounces Ceres peach juice

- **9½ ounces Hendrick's Gin**

- **¼ ounce Fee Brothers Peach Bitters**

Combine → Place the ingredients in a medium-size metal bowl and stir.

Freeze → Pour the liquid into a large freezer bag and place it in the freezer until frozen, approximately 4 hours. Alternatively, pour the liquid into an ice cream maker and proceed per the manufacturer's instructions (see page 11).

Serve → When you're ready to drink, massage the freezer bag by hand until it's a wet, slushy consistency. If it's not breaking up, run the bag quickly under hot water and massage some more.

Yield → Makes at least 4 drinks.

CITRUS BLITZ

Sometimes you don't need any spirits to lift your spirits. Make your nonimbibing friends happy at your next party with this bright and zesty frozen blend of grapefruit, pineapple, and lime.

ABV
0%

GLASS
Flared

GARNISH
candied grapefruit peel

- ½ ounce water
- 8¼ ounces Simple Syrup (page 18)
- 3 ounces lime juice
- 14¼ ounces grapefruit juice
- 14¼ ounces pineapple juice

Combine → Place the ingredients in a medium-size metal bowl and stir.

Freeze → Pour the liquid into a large freezer bag and place it in the freezer until frozen, approximately 4 hours. Alternatively, pour the liquid into an ice cream maker and proceed per the manufacturer's instructions (see page 11).

Serve → When you're ready to drink, massage the freezer bag by hand until it's a wet, slushy consistency. If it's not breaking up, run the bag quickly under hot water and massage some more.

Yield → Makes at least 4 drinks.

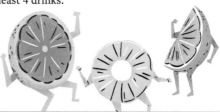

DO THE TWIST!

Want to make perfect citrus peel twists for all of your drinks? Grab a citrus stripper or zester (OXO brand is a good one) and work it around the outside of the citrus fruit, peeling off just the outside of the peel (not the white part). After a little practice, you'll be able to create a perfect ribbon twist to drape on many of your cocktails.

SWEET

fetch
(page 87)

the elphaba
(page 73)

cool hand luke
(page 68)

gose in the shell
(page 67)

THE POM-POM

These two gingers (red-headed pomegranate liqueur and real ginger Domaine de Canton) will dance across your taste buds, rallying the troops for a night on the town.

ABV
5.89%

GLASS
Flared

GARNISH
candied ginger, black pom-pom stencil (see page 23)

pom-pom stencil

- 2¾ ounces water
- 12 ounces Simple Syrup (page 18)
- 8 ounces lemon juice
- 7¾ ounces lime juice
- 3¼ ounces PAMA Pomegranate Liqueur
- 6½ ounces Domaine de Canton Ginger Liqueur

Combine → Place the ingredients in a medium-size metal bowl and stir.

Freeze → Pour the liquid into a large freezer bag and place it in the freezer until frozen, approximately 4 hours. Alternatively, pour the liquid into an ice cream maker and proceed per the manufacturer's instructions (see page 11).

Serve → When you're ready to drink, massage the freezer bag by hand until it's a wet, slushy consistency. If it's not breaking up, run the bag quickly under hot water and massage some more.

Yield → Makes at least 4 drinks.

BLUE ROSES

We have tricks in our pockets; we have blue Curaçao up our sleeves. Our homage to *The Glass Menagerie* is a fragile combination of sweet orange and a hint of rose hip—it'll really blow out your candles.

ABV
5.75%

GLASS
Floral Bowl

GARNISH
candied grapefruit peel, a glass unicorn, and Tennessee Williams

- 7¼ ounces Simple Syrup (page 18)
- 2¼ ounces Genuine Blue Curaçao Liqueur
- 8¾ ounces Koval Rose Hip Liqueur
- 21¾ ounces whole milk

Combine → Place the Simple Syrup, Curaçao, and rose hip liqueur in a medium-size metal bowl and stir.

Blend → Add the milk to the bowl slowly, using an immersion blender to emulsify the mixture.

Freeze → Pour the liquid into a large freezer bag and place it in the freezer until frozen, approximately 4 hours. Alternatively, pour the liquid into an ice cream maker and proceed per the manufacturer's instructions (see page 11).

Serve → When you're ready to drink, massage the freezer bag by hand until it's a wet, slushy consistency. If it's not breaking up, run the bag quickly under hot water and massage some more.

Yield → Makes at least 4 drinks.

ORANGE JULIO

No Julius here (our lawyers said no), but you get our drift. This smooth, creamy frozen variation on orangecello is one you'll want to keep for yourself.

ABV
6.42%

GLASS
Rippled

GARNISH
orange twist

- 5 ounces Simple Syrup (page 18)
- 19½ ounces orange juice
- **2½ ounces Tito's Handmade Vodka**
- **5 ounces Caravella Orangecello Originale**
- 8½ ounces whole milk

Combine → Place the simple syrup, orange juice, vodka, and orangecello in a medium-size metal bowl and stir.

Blend → Add the milk to the bowl slowly, using an immersion blender to emulsify the mixture.

Freeze → Pour the liquid into a large freezer bag and place it in the freezer until frozen, approximately 4 hours. Alternatively, pour the liquid into an ice cream maker and proceed per the manufacturer's instructions (see page 11).

Serve → When you're ready to drink, massage the freezer bag by hand until it's a wet, slushy consistency. If it's not breaking up, run the bag quickly under hot water and massage some more.

Yield → Makes at least 4 drinks.

SAILOR'S GOLD

Ahoy! You may not be able to find the treasure after drinking this combo of spiced rum, orange liqueur, and fresh juices, but you probably won't care.

ABV
11.8%

GLASS
Flared

GARNISH
candied orange peel, fresh cherry, and *Pirates of the Caribbean*

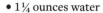

- 1¼ ounces water
- 3¾ ounces Simple Syrup (page 18)
- 3¾ ounces lemon juice
- 16 ounces orange juice
- 4¾ ounces pineapple juice
- **6 ounces Sailor Jerry Spiced Rum**
- **4¾ ounces Gran Gala Triple Orange Liqueur**

Combine → Place the ingredients in a medium-size metal bowl and stir.

Freeze → Pour the liquid into a large freezer bag and place it in the freezer until frozen, approximately 4 hours. Alternatively, pour the liquid into an ice cream maker and proceed per the manufacturer's instructions (see page 11).

Serve → When you're ready to drink, massage the freezer bag by hand until it's a wet, slushy consistency. If it's not breaking up, run the bag quickly under hot water and massage some more.

Yield → Makes at least 4 drinks.

BANANARAMA

It was a cruel, cruel summer, leaving us here all alone in the banana stand. We came up with this to bide the time. Hints of orange and vanilla from the brandy-based Tuaca tickle your taste buds after the chocolate and banana have washed away.

ABV
15.59%

GLASS
Round & Round

GARNISH
banana slices on a skewer with a drizzle of Torani Dark Chocolate Sauce

- 3½ ounces water
- 5¼ **ounces 99 Bananas Liqueur**
- 3½ **ounces 360 Double Chocolate Vodka**
- 7 **ounces Tuaca Vanilla Citrus Liqueur**
- 21 ounces whole milk

Combine → Place the water, banana liqueur, vodka, and tuaca liqueur in a medium-size metal bowl and stir.

Blend → Add the milk to the bowl slowly, using an immersion blender to emulsify the mixture.

Freeze → Pour the liquid into a large freezer bag and place it in the freezer until frozen, approximately 4 hours. Alternatively, pour the liquid into an ice cream maker and proceed per the manufacturer's instructions (see page 11).

Serve → When you're ready to drink, massage the freezer bag by hand until it's a wet, slushy consistency. If it's not breaking up, run the bag quickly under hot water and massage some more.

Yield → Makes at least 4 drinks.

JAM ON IT

Our mama gave us a brand new toy: two liquors to bring you joy. Chambord and gin need no encore, but add a touch of lemon here, and you'll have a riff on a frozen Bramble.

ABV
10.44%

GLASS
Flared

GARNISH
fresh raspberries

- 20 ounces water

- 7½ ounces Simple Syrup (page 18)

- **4¼ ounces Chambord Liqueur**

- **8½ ounces Plymouth Gin**

Combine → Place the ingredients in a medium-size metal bowl and stir.

Freeze → Pour the liquid into a large freezer bag and place it in the freezer until frozen, approximately 4 hours. Alternatively, pour the liquid into an ice cream maker and proceed per the manufacturer's instructions (see page 11).

Serve → When you're ready to drink, massage the freezer bag by hand until it's a wet, slushy consistency. If it's not breaking up, run the bag quickly under hot water and massage some more.

Yield → Makes at least 4 drinks.

CHOCOLATE-COVERED STRAWBERRY

Anyone can bring their true love a strawberry dipped in milk chocolate, but only you can craft a frozen drink that tastes like one.

ABV
6.18%

GLASS
Flared

GARNISH
sugar rim, dark cocoa powder lattice stencil

- 7¾ ounces Strawberry Simple Syrup (page 19)
- **5½ ounces Strawberry-Infused Tito's Vodka (page 20)**
- **3¾ ounces Thatcher's Organic Dark Chocolate Liqueur**
- 20 ounces whole milk
- 3¼ ounces Torani Dark Chocolate Sauce

Combine → Place the simple syrup, vodka, and dark chocolate liqueur in a medium-size metal bowl and stir.

Blend → Combine the milk and the chocolate sauce and add them to the bowl slowly, using an immersion blender to emulsify the mixture.

Freeze → Pour the liquid into a large freezer bag and place it in the freezer until frozen, approximately 4 hours. Alternatively, pour the liquid into an ice cream maker and proceed per the manufacturer's instructions (see page 11).

Serve → When you're ready to drink, massage the freezer bag by hand until it's a wet, slushy consistency. If it's not breaking up, run the bag quickly under hot water and massage some more.

Yield → Makes at least 4 drinks.

LAUNCHPAD MCQUACK

Technically, Launchpad McQuack is not really the name of this drink, but we've always wanted a beverage named after our favorite cartoon duck pilot. What we have here is a Cold Hot Chocolate. The infused cinnamon will warm up your taste buds while the temperature cools you down.

ABV
5.09%

GLASS
Coffreeze & Teas

GARNISH
powdered sugar lattice stencil

- 5 ounces Simple Syrup (page 18)
- **2½ ounces Cinnamon-Infused Tito's Vodka (page 20)**
- **5 ounces Godiva Milk Chocolate Liqueur**
- 21½ ounces whole milk
- **2½ ounces Baileys Irish Cream**
- 3¾ ounces Torani Dark Chocolate Sauce

Combine → Place the simple syrup, vodka, and milk chocolate liqueur in a medium-size metal bowl and stir.

Blend → Combine the milk, Baileys, and chocolate sauce, and add them to the bowl slowly, using an immersion blender to emulsify the mixture.

Freeze → Pour the liquid into a large freezer bag and place it in the freezer until frozen, approximately 4 hours. Alternatively, pour the liquid into an ice cream maker and proceed per the manufacturer's instructions (see page 11).

Serve → When you're ready to drink, massage the freezer bag by hand until it's a wet, slushy consistency. If it's not breaking up, run the bag quickly under hot water and massage some more.

Yield → Makes at least 4 drinks.

FLOATY MCFLOAT FACE

Skip the ice cream and insert the Buffalo Trace Bourbon and a touch of Baileys for an adult twist on this kids' classic.

ABV
12.66%

GLASS
Flared

GARNISH
malted milk balls

- 23¼ ounces Whole Foods 365 Root Beer
- **5 ounces Buffalo Trace Kentucky Straight Bourbon Whiskey**
- 10 ounces whole milk
- **1¾ ounces Baileys Irish Cream**

Combine → Place the root beer and bourbon in a medium-size metal bowl and stir.

Blend → Combine the milk and the Baileys and add them to the bowl slowly, using an immersion blender to emulsify the mixture. (It will foam!)

Freeze → Pour the liquid into a large freezer bag and place it in the freezer until frozen, approximately 4 hours. Alternatively, pour the liquid into an ice cream maker and proceed per the manufacturer's instructions (see page 11).

Serve → When you're ready to drink, massage the freezer bag by hand until it's a wet, slushy consistency. If it's not breaking up, run the bag quickly under hot water and massage some more.

Yield → Makes at least 4 drinks.

THE JOY OF ALMOND

Candy bars are best boozy and through a straw. So get off your couch and mix up some amaretto and chocolate vodka.

ABV
7.91%

GLASS
Flared

GARNISH
chocolate shavings and shredded coconut

- 13½ ounces Simple Syrup (page 18)
- **4¾ ounces Trader Vic's Amaretto Liqueur**
- **5½ ounces 360 Double Chocolate Vodka**
- 16½ ounces whole milk

Combine → Place the simple syrup, amaretto liqueur, and chocolate vodka in a medium-size metal bowl and stir.

Blend → Add the milk to the bowl slowly, using an immersion blender to emulsify the mixture.

Freeze → Pour the liquid into a large freezer bag and place it in the freezer until frozen, approximately 4 hours. Alternatively, pour the liquid into an ice cream maker and proceed per the manufacturer's instructions (see page 11).

Serve → When you're ready to drink, massage the freezer bag by hand until it's a wet, slushy consistency. If it's not breaking up, run the bag quickly under hot water and massage some more.

Yield → Makes at least 4 drinks.

O'MALLEY'S RENDEZVOUS

If you like piña coladas and getting caught in the rain, you might try this old drink that you thought was too plain. For your friends who love the classics, a little pineapple, coconut, and two types of rum will start your beach party off right.

ABV
10.48%

GLASS
Rippled

GARNISH
pineapple and orange skewer

- 7 ounces Coco López Cream of Coconut
- 14¼ ounces pineapple juice
- **4½ ounces Sailor Jerry Spiced Rum**
- **4½ ounces Bacardi White Rum**
- **1¾ ounces Crème de Cassis**
- 8¼ ounces whole milk

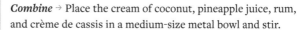

Combine → Place the cream of coconut, pineapple juice, rum, and crème de cassis in a medium-size metal bowl and stir.

Blend → Add the milk to the bowl slowly, using an immersion blender to emulsify the mixture.

Freeze → Pour the liquid into a large freezer bag and place it in the freezer until frozen, approximately 4 hours. Alternatively, pour the liquid into an ice cream maker and proceed per the manufacturer's instructions (see page 11).

Serve → When you're ready to drink, massage the freezer bag by hand until it's a wet, slushy consistency. If it's not breaking up, run the bag quickly under hot water and massage some more.

Yield → Makes at least 4 drinks.

KANSAS CITY KICKER

Our take on the frozen Horsefeather—ginger beer, lemon, and whiskey. Although you can swap in your own local favorites, our original is crafted with KC legends like Boulevard Brewing Company's Ginger Lemon Radler, Kansas City Canning Company's shrub, and J. Rieger whiskey.

ABV
11.9%

GLASS
Up & Down

GARNISH
candied ginger and lemon twist

- ¾ ounce water
- 6¼ ounces Simple Syrup (page 18)
- 1¾ ounces lemon juice
- 4½ ounces Kansas City Canning Co. Blood Orange Ginger Shrub
- **17 ounces Boulevard Ginger Lemon Radler Beer**
- **2½ ounces Caravella Limoncello Originale**
- **7¼ ounces J. Rieger & Co. Whiskey**

Combine → Place the ingredients in a medium-size metal bowl and stir.

Freeze → Pour the liquid into a large freezer bag and place it in the freezer until frozen, approximately 4 hours. Alternatively, pour the liquid into an ice cream maker and proceed per the manufacturer's instructions (see page 11).

Serve → When you're ready to drink, massage the freezer bag by hand until it's a wet, slushy consistency. If it's not breaking up, run the bag quickly under hot water and massage some more.

Yield → Makes at least 4 drinks.

PERFECTO ROBERTO

In *The Joy of Mixology*, author Gary Regan refers to being unable to make a Rob Roy in frozen form. We accepted this challenge. Freezing initially tames the Glenfiddich, but it comes back to life on your palate as it warms. We hope we make Regan proud.

ABV
9.65%

GLASS
Round & Round

GARNISH
lemon twist with a side of frozen-cocktail-making ego

- 20 ounces water
- 8¼ ounces Simple Syrup (page 18)
- **1¾ ounces Cinzano Extra Dry Vermouth**
- **1¾ ounces Cinzano Rosso Sweet Vermouth**
- **8¼ ounces Glenfiddich Single Malt Scotch Whiskey**
- **¼ teaspoon Peychaud's Bitters**

Combine → Place the ingredients in a medium-size metal bowl and stir.

Freeze → Pour the liquid into a large freezer bag and place it in the freezer until frozen, approximately 4 hours. Alternatively, pour the liquid into an ice cream maker and proceed per the manufacturer's instructions (see page 11).

Serve → When you're ready to drink, massage the freezer bag by hand until it's a wet, slushy consistency. If it's not breaking up, run the bag quickly under hot water and massage some more.

Yield → Makes at least 4 drinks.

HEMINGWAY'S JAZZ

Another riff on the daiquiri in honor of Hemingway (see page 43 for the first one). Here we include the drier maraschino liqueur in lieu of the floral hibiscus.

ABV
8.63%

GLASS
Floral Bowl

GARNISH
grapefruit twist, book stencil (see page 23)

book stencil

- 1¼ ounces water

- 4¾ ounces Simple Syrup (page 18)

- 8 ounces lime juice

- 7¾ ounces grapefruit juice

- **7¾ ounces Bacardi White Rum**

- **1¾ ounces Luxardo Maraschino Liqueur**

- 9½ ounces whole milk

Combine → Place the water, simple syrup, lime juice, grapefruit juice, rum, and maraschino liqueur in a medium-size metal bowl and stir.

Blend → Add the milk to the bowl slowly, using an immersion blender to emulsify the mixture.

Freeze → Pour the liquid into a large freezer bag and place it in the freezer until frozen, approximately 4 hours. Alternatively, pour the liquid into an ice cream maker and proceed per the manufacturer's instructions (see page 11).

Serve → When you're ready to drink, massage the freezer bag by hand until it's a wet, slushy consistency. If it's not breaking up, run the bag quickly under hot water and massage some more.

Yield → Makes at least 4 drinks.

THE O'CONNELL

When Snow & Co. first started, one of our patrons asked if we made a whiskey slush. We didn't, so he offered up his grandfather's recipe. This Jameson slush, courtesy of Grandpa O'Connell, wouldn't actually freeze the first few times we made it because it was too strong. This recalibrated version is still a knockout of a drink!

ABV
12.43%

GLASS
Up & Down

GARNISH
orange peel

- 7¼ ounces water
- 4½ ounces Simple Syrup (page 18)
- 8½ ounces Tazo Iced True Black Tea (steeped)
- 6¼ ounces orange juice
- 2¾ ounces lemon juice
- **11 ounces Jameson Irish Whiskey**

Combine → Place the ingredients in a medium-size metal bowl and stir.

Freeze → Pour the liquid into a large freezer bag and place it in the freezer until frozen, approximately 4 hours. Alternatively, pour the liquid into an ice cream maker and proceed per the manufacturer's instructions (see page 11).

Serve → When you're ready to drink, massage the freezer bag by hand until it's a wet, slushy consistency. If it's not breaking up, run the bag quickly under hot water and massage some more.

Yield → Makes at least 4 drinks.

GOSE IN THE SHELL

Get hacked by this triangulation of Tito's vodka, Gose beer, and hibiscus liqueur. Is it a shandy? A frozen flower? Maybe you are a frozen cocktail and it is drinking you.

ABV
6.94%

GLASS
Pils & Chills

GARNISH
hibiscus flower

- 2½ ounces water

- 7 ounces Simple Syrup (page 18)

- 7 ounces lemon juice

- **16½ ounces Boulevard Hibiscus Gose Beer**

- **3¼ ounces Tito's Handmade Vodka**

- **4 ounces Fruit Lab Hibiscus Liqueur**

Combine → Place the ingredients in a medium-size metal bowl and stir.

Freeze → Pour the liquid into a large freezer bag and place it in the freezer until frozen, approximately 4 hours. Alternatively, pour the liquid into an ice cream maker and proceed per the manufacturer's instructions (see page 11).

Serve → When you're ready to drink, massage the freezer bag by hand until it's a wet, slushy consistency. If it's not breaking up, run the bag quickly under hot water and massage some more.

Yield → Makes at least 4 drinks.

COOL HAND LUKE

This cuke-heavy citrus blast with a splash of Pimm's Blackberry will bring new meaning to being a cool cucumber.

ABV
5.68%

GLASS
Floral Bowl

GARNISH
cucumber wheel

- 2 ounces water
- 9½ ounces Simple Syrup (page 18)
- 4 ounces lemon juice
- 2¾ ounces lime juice
- **2¼ ounces Pimm's Blackberry & Elderflower**
- **12¼ ounces Thatcher's Organic Cucumber Liqueur**
- 7½ ounces whole milk

Combine → Place the water, simple syrup, lemon juice, lime juice, Pimm's, and cucumber liqueur in a medium-size metal bowl and stir.

Blend → Add the milk to the bowl slowly, using an immersion blender to emulsify the mixture.

Freeze → Pour the liquid into a large freezer bag and place it in the freezer until frozen, approximately 4 hours. Alternatively, pour the liquid into an ice cream maker and proceed per the manufacturer's instructions (see page 11).

Serve → When you're ready to drink, massage the freezer bag by hand until it's a wet, slushy consistency. If it's not breaking up, run the bag quickly under hot water and massage some more.

Yield → Makes at least 4 drinks.

BUTTERED UP

Muggles, beware: This sweet buttery mix of butterscotch Schnapps, two flavored vodkas, and Tuaca is not for the youngsters. And certainly not to be mixed with flying on a broom.

ABV
10.38%

GLASS
Flared

GARNISH
whipped cream and spices

- 4¼ ounces Simple Syrup (page 18)
- **½ ounce Angostura Bitters**
- **7¼ ounces Boulaine Butterscotch Schnapps**
- **1¼ ounces 360 Glazed Donut Vodka**
- **2½ ounces 360 Madagascar Vanilla Vodka**
- **5 ounces Tuaca Vanilla Citrus Liqueur**
- 19¼ ounces whole milk

Combine → Place the simple syrup, Angostura bitters, butterscotch schnapps, glazed donut vodka, vanilla vodka, and Tuaca liqueur in a medium-size metal bowl and stir.

Blend → Add the milk to the bowl slowly, using an immersion blender to emulsify the mixture.

Freeze → Pour the liquid into a large freezer bag and place it in the freezer until frozen, approximately 4 hours. Alternatively, pour the liquid into an ice cream maker and proceed per the manufacturer's instructions (see page 11).

Serve → When you're ready to drink, massage the freezer bag by hand until it's a wet, slushy consistency. If it's not breaking up, run the bag quickly under hot water and massage some more.

Yield → Makes at least 4 drinks.

BETTER THAN BEADS

Our variation on the classic hurricane from the Big Easy, and a classy antidote to those cheap beads you have around your neck. . . .

ABV
9.8%

GLASS
Rippled

GARNISH
fresh cherries, Mardi Gras beads

- 19¾ ounces water
- 8¼ ounces Simple Syrup (page 18)
- ¾ ounce Crème de Banana
- 2½ ounces Bacardi White Rum
- 2½ ounces Sailor Jerry Spiced Rum
- 2½ ounces X-Rated Fusion Liqueur
- 2½ ounces PAMA Pomegranate Liqueur
- 1¼ ounces Luxardo Maraschino Liqueur
- ¼ teaspoon Angostura Bitters

Combine → Place the ingredients in a medium-size metal bowl and stir.

Freeze → Pour the liquid into a large freezer bag and place it in the freezer until frozen, approximately 4 hours. Alternatively, pour the liquid into an ice cream maker and proceed per the manufacturer's instructions (see page 11).

Serve → When you're ready to drink, massage the freezer bag by hand until it's a wet, slushy consistency. If it's not breaking up, run the bag quickly under hot water and massage some more.

Yield → Makes at least 4 drinks.

PB & J

Do you like to drink your lunch? Give this PB & J a try. We were a bit skeptical the first time we put peanuts in vodka, but trust us . . . it's worth it.

ABV
7.59%

GLASS
Round & Round

GARNISH
honey-roasted peanuts

- 7½ ounces Simple Syrup (page 18)
- **5 ounces Honey-Roasted Peanut–Infused Tito's Vodka (page 21)**
- **6½ ounces Chambord Liqueur**
- 19¾ ounces whole milk
- 1¾ ounces all-natural peanut butter

Combine → Place the simple syrup, vodka, and Chambord liqueur in a medium-size metal bowl and stir.

Blend → Combine the milk and the peanut butter and add them to the bowl slowly, using an immersion blender to emulsify the mixture.

Freeze → Pour the liquid into a large freezer bag and place it in the freezer until frozen, approximately 4 hours. Alternatively, pour the liquid into an ice cream maker and proceed per the manufacturer's instructions (see page 11).

Serve → When you're ready to drink, massage the freezer bag by hand until it's a wet, slushy consistency. If it's not breaking up, run the bag quickly under hot water and massage some more.

Yield → Makes at least 4 drinks.

A KICK TO THE PEACHES

Lavender-infused simple syrup sets off this traditional peach Bellini. Sweet and smooth, but don't let that fool you—it's got booze in there.

ABV
5.07%

GLASS
Bubbles Bubbles

GARNISH
lavender sprig, gold luster-dusted peach slice (see page 24)

- 13¼ ounces water
- 11¼ ounces Lavender Simple Syrup (page 19)
- 6¾ ounces Stellina Di Notte Prosecco
- 8¾ ounces Stirrings Peach Liqueur

Combine → Place the ingredients in a medium-size metal bowl and stir.

Freeze → Pour the liquid into a large freezer bag and place it in the freezer until frozen, approximately 4 hours. Alternatively, pour the liquid into an ice cream maker and proceed per the manufacturer's instructions (see page 11).

Serve → When you're ready to drink, massage the freezer bag by hand until it's a wet, slushy consistency. If it's not breaking up, run the bag quickly under hot water and massage some more.

Yield → Makes at least 4 drinks.

THE ELPHABA

With this drink at your next party, you won't need Glinda to make you feel popular. A twist on A Kick to the Peaches, left, this variation subs in Midori melon liqueur for some of the peach.

ABV
6.79%

GLASS
Bubbles Bubbles

GARNISH
black witch hat stencil (see page 23)

- 13¼ ounces water
- 11¼ ounces Simple Syrup (page 18)
- **6¾ ounces Stellina Di Notte Prosecco**
- **2¼ ounces Stirrings Peach Liqueur**
- **6¾ ounces Midori Melon Liqueur**

witch hat stencil

Combine → Place the ingredients in a medium-size metal bowl and stir.

Freeze → Pour the liquid into a large freezer bag and place it in the freezer until frozen, approximately 4 hours. Alternatively, pour the liquid into an ice cream maker and proceed per the manufacturer's instructions (see page 11).

Serve → When you're ready to drink, massage the freezer bag by hand until it's a wet, slushy consistency. If it's not breaking up, run the bag quickly under hot water and massage some more.

Yield → Makes at least 4 drinks.

THINLY MINTED

A little mint to relax the nerves pairs well with chocolate as a reward for that long work week. Elegant and simple—just like those Girl Scout cookies that you're keeping in the freezer.

ABV
5.07%

GLASS
Coffreeze & Teas

GARNISH
mint leaf stencil, (see page 23) mint sprig, crumbled chocolate cookie rim

- 6 ounces Simple Syrup (page 18)
- **5¼ ounces Crème de Menthe**
- 17½ ounces whole milk
- **7 ounces Baileys Irish Cream**
- 4½ ounces Torani Dark Chocolate Sauce

mint leaf stencil

Combine → Place the simple syrup and crème de menthe in a medium-size metal bowl and stir.

Blend → Combine the milk, Baileys, and chocolate sauce, and add them to the bowl slowly, using an immersion blender to emulsify the mixture.

Freeze → Pour the liquid into a large freezer bag and place it in the freezer until frozen, approximately 4 hours. Alternatively, pour the liquid into an ice cream maker and proceed per the manufacturer's instructions (see page 11).

Serve → When you're ready to drink, massage the freezer bag by hand until it's a wet, slushy consistency. If it's not breaking up, run the bag quickly under hot water and massage some more.

Yield → Makes at least 4 drinks.

THE DUDE

The Dude abides and so does this drink. A frozen white Russian elevated with vanilla vodka, Kahlúa, Baileys, and Frangelico hazelnut liqueur. Be careful, man, there's a beverage here.

ABV
8.07%

GLASS
Up & Down

GARNISH
cinnamon stick and a bathrobe (for you)

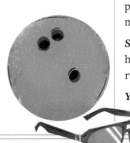

- 11¼ ounces Simple Syrup (page 18)
- **3¼ ounces Frangelico Liqueur**
- **3¼ ounces Kahlúa**
- **3¼ ounces 360 Madagascar Vanilla Vodka**
- 15½ ounces whole milk
- **3¼ ounces Baileys Irish Cream**

Combine → Place the simple syrup, Frangelico liqueur, Kahlúa, and vanilla vodka in a medium-size metal bowl and stir.

Blend → Combine the milk and the Baileys and add them to the bowl slowly, using an immersion blender to emulsify the mixture.

Freeze → Pour the liquid into a large freezer bag and place it in the freezer until frozen, approximately 4 hours. Alternatively, pour the liquid into an ice cream maker and proceed per the manufacturer's instructions (see page 11).

Serve → When you're ready to drink, massage the freezer bag by hand until it's a wet, slushy consistency. If it's not breaking up, run the bag quickly under hot water and massage some more.

Yield → Makes at least 4 drinks.

THE COCOMO

Wanna get away from it all? Tame that tequila with some sweet and tropical mango. The milk blended in will soften the edge.

ABV
10.34%

GLASS
Rippled

GARNISH
mango chunk

- 4¼ ounces water
- 25 ounces Ceres Mango fruit juice
- **7½ ounces Herradura Añejo Tequila**
- 3¼ ounces whole milk

Combine → Place the water, mango juice, and tequila in a medium-size metal bowl and stir.

Blend → Add the milk to the bowl slowly, using an immersion blender to emulsify the mixture.

Freeze → Pour the liquid into a large freezer bag and place it in the freezer until frozen, approximately 4 hours. Alternatively, pour the liquid into an ice cream maker and proceed per the manufacturer's instructions (see page 11).

Serve → When you're ready to drink, massage the freezer bag by hand until it's a wet, slushy consistency. If it's not breaking up, run the bag quickly under hot water and massage some more.

Yield → Makes at least 4 drinks.

BLUE BELLS

We're big fans of Chambord raspberry liqueur, and it gets to shine through in this drink. The tang of apricot liqueur and some bitterness from the Suze help take the sweetness down a notch for a unique flavor.

ABV
7.04%

GLASS
Floral Bowl

GARNISH
blueberries on a skewer

- 12½ ounces Simple Syrup (page 18)
- **4½ ounces Rothman & Winter Orchard Apricot Liqueur**
- **1¾ ounces Suze Aperitif Liqueur**
- **8½ ounces Chambord Liqueur**
- 13 ounces whole milk

Combine → Place the simple syrup, apricot liqueur, aperitif liqueur, and Chambord liqueur in a medium-size metal bowl and stir.

Blend → Add the milk to the bowl slowly, using an immersion blender to emulsify the mixture.

Freeze → Pour the liquid into a large freezer bag and place it in the freezer until frozen, approximately 4 hours. Alternatively, pour the liquid into an ice cream maker and proceed per the manufacturer's instructions (see page 11).

Serve → When you're ready to drink, massage the freezer bag by hand until it's a wet, slushy consistency. If it's not breaking up, run the bag quickly under hot water and massage some more.

Yield → Makes at least 4 drinks.

BOURBON AND BERRIES

Time for dessert? Skip the strawberry shortcake and opt for this creamy dreamy strawberry and bourbon cocktail instead.

ABV
8.98%

GLASS
Up & Down

GARNISH
strawberry slices

- 12½ ounces Strawberry Simple Syrup (page 19)
- **1 ounce Strawberry-Infused Tito's Vodka (page 20)**
- **7¼ ounces Buffalo Trace Kentucky Straight Bourbon Whiskey**
- 19½ ounces whole milk

Combine → Place the simple syrup, vodka, and bourbon in a medium-size metal bowl and stir.

Blend → Add the milk to the bowl slowly, using an immersion blender to emulsify the mixture.

Freeze → Pour the liquid into a large freezer bag and place it in the freezer until frozen, approximately 4 hours. Alternatively, pour the liquid into an ice cream maker and proceed per the manufacturer's instructions (see page 11).

Serve → When you're ready to drink, massage the freezer bag by hand until it's a wet, slushy consistency. If it's not breaking up, run the bag quickly under hot water and massage some more.

Yield → Makes at least 4 drinks.

PURPLE RAIN

A transcendent mix of sweet raspberry and blueberry with a velvety smooth texture, this frozen berry blast is one of our all-time best-sellers at Snow & Co. Take our word for it: There's booze in there, and if you don't believe us, ask one of our patrons.

ABV
6.6%

GLASS
Flared

GARNISH
infused blueberries from moonshine on skewer

- 13¾ ounces Simple Syrup (page 18)
- **3¼ ounces Junior Johnson Midnight Moon Blueberry Infused Moonshine**
- **6¼ ounces Chambord Liqueur**
- 17 ounces whole milk

Combine → Place the simple syrup, moonshine, and Chambord liqueur in a medium-size metal bowl and stir.

Blend → Add the milk to the bowl slowly, using an immersion blender to emulsify the mixture.

Freeze → Pour the liquid into a large freezer bag and place it in the freezer until frozen, approximately 4 hours. Alternatively, pour the liquid into an ice cream maker and proceed per the manufacturer's instructions (see page 11).

Serve → When you're ready to drink, massage the freezer bag by hand until it's a wet, slushy consistency. If it's not breaking up, run the bag quickly under hot water and massage some more.

Yield → Makes at least 4 drinks.

BLACK VELVET

A new frozen religion based on the unusual combination of Guinness stout and prosecco. Chocolate vodka accentuates the already chocolaty notes of the Guinness.

ABV
6.21%

GLASS
Pils & Chills

GARNISH
wavy line stencil
(see page 23)

wavy line stencil

- 12½ ounces water

- 10¾ ounces Simple Syrup (page 18)

- **8 ounces Stellina Di Notte Prosecco**

- **4¾ ounces Guinness Stout**

- **4 ounces 360 Double Chocolate Vodka**

Combine → Place the ingredients in a medium-size metal bowl and stir.

Freeze → Pour the liquid into a large freezer bag and place it in the freezer until frozen, approximately 4 hours. Alternatively, pour the liquid into an ice cream maker and proceed per the manufacturer's instructions (see page 11).

Serve → When you're ready to drink, massage the freezer bag by hand until it's a wet, slushy consistency. If it's not breaking up, run the bag quickly under hot water and massage some more.

Yield → Makes at least 4 drinks.

AUNTIE'S FRUITCAKE

Over the holidays, many households are beset with a cornucopia of well-intentioned baked goods. But here's a fruitcake that you won't want to regift. Cinnamon and ginger from the Domaine de Canton play up just a touch of pineapple sweetness.

ABV
9.31%

GLASS
Round & Round

GARNISH
pineapple chunks on a skewer

- ¾ ounce water
- 2 ounces Simple Syrup (page 18)
- 5 ounces Cinnamon-Infused Simple Syrup (page 19)
- 2 ounces lemon juice
- 10 ounces pineapple juice
- **7½ ounces Olmeca Altos Reposado Tequila**
- **2½ ounces Domaine de Canton Ginger Liqueur**
- 10 ounces whole milk

Combine → Place the water, simple syrups, juices, tequila, and ginger liqueur in a medium-size metal bowl and stir.

Blend → Add the milk to the bowl slowly, using an immersion blender to emulsify the mixture.

Freeze → Pour the liquid into a large freezer bag and place it in the freezer until frozen, approximately 4 hours. Alternatively, pour the liquid into an ice cream maker and proceed per the manufacturer's instructions (see page 11).

Serve → When you're ready to drink, massage the freezer bag by hand until it's a wet, slushy consistency. If it's not breaking up, run the bag quickly under hot water and massage some more.

Yield → Makes at least 4 drinks.

NIGHTTIME JOE

Cram for your next test (literal or metaphorical) with this cold, booze-filled brew and you'll ace any question in your path. Sweet yet strong.

ABV
11.8%

GLASS
Coffreeze & Teas

GARNISH
whole coffee beans

- 1¾ ounces lemon juice
- 4¼ ounces Honey Syrup (page 18)
- **10½ ounces Grind Espresso Spirit**
- **4¼ ounces Coffee Bean–Infused Bulleit Bourbon Frontier Whiskey (page 22)**
- 22 ounces whole milk

Combine → Place the lemon juice, honey syrup, espresso spirit, and whiskey in a medium-size metal bowl and stir.

Blend → Add the milk to the bowl slowly, using an immersion blender to emulsify the mixture.

Freeze → Pour the liquid into a large freezer bag and place it in the freezer until frozen, approximately 4 hours. Alternatively, pour the liquid into an ice cream maker and proceed per the manufacturer's instructions (see page 11).

Serve → When you're ready to drink, massage the freezer bag by hand until it's a wet, slushy consistency. If it's not breaking up, run the bag quickly under hot water and massage some more.

Yield → Makes at least 4 drinks.

BARISTA LIFE

When baristas have fever dreams, they grab this elixir to cool down. Start with coffee-infused bourbon, add a little more coffee, then round it out with two distinct flavors of orange.

ABV
9.91%

GLASS
Coffreeze & Teas

GARNISH
orange wheel

- 7 ounces Simple Syrup (page 18)

- 11¾ ounces orange juice

- 11¾ ounces freshly brewed coffee

- **¼ ounce Fee Brothers Orange Bitters**

- **9½ ounces Coffee Bean–Infused Bulleit Bourbon Frontier Whiskey (page 22)**

Combine → Place the ingredients in a medium-size metal bowl and stir.

Freeze → Pour the liquid into a large freezer bag and place it in the freezer until frozen, approximately 4 hours. Alternatively, pour the liquid into an ice cream maker and proceed per the manufacturer's instructions (see page 11).

Serve → When you're ready to drink, massage the freezer bag by hand until it's a wet, slushy consistency. If it's not breaking up, run the bag quickly under hot water and massage some more.

Yield → Makes at least 4 drinks.

GIN FO'SHIZZLE

Snoop hasn't taken us up on trying this when he's come through KC, but we dream this is what he'd say after tasting it. Crisp and clean, this frozen gin fizz made with Missouri's fine Pinckney Bend Gin and lemon tonic is a great choice for any occasion.

ABV
8.34%

GLASS
Floral Bowl

GARNISH
gold luster dust bubble stencil (see page 23)

- 1¼ ounces water
- 4½ ounces Simple Syrup (page 18)
- 4½ ounces lemon juice
- 4 ounces orange juice
- 17½ ounces Fever-Tree Bitter Lemon Tonic
- **8½ ounces Pinckney Bend Gin**

bubble stencil

Combine → Place the ingredients in a medium-size metal bowl and stir.

Freeze → Pour the liquid into a large freezer bag and place it in the freezer until frozen, approximately 4 hours. Alternatively, pour the liquid into an ice cream maker and proceed per the manufacturer's instructions (see page 11).

Serve → When you're ready to drink, massage the freezer bag by hand until it's a wet, slusvhy consistency. If it's not breaking up, run the bag quickly under hot water and massage some more.

Yield → Makes at least 4 drinks.

FIELD OF DREAMS

Part of the frozen shandy family, this sweet yet aromatic sipper uses Boulevard Brewing's Tank 7 Farmhouse Ale, a light-bodied but boozy ale (and a solid drinking choice all by itself), paired with peach and the juniper from the gin. You can imagine taking a break from a hard day in the field with this cool concoction.

ABV
7.48%

GLASS
Pils & Chills

GARNISH
peach slice on a skewer, and the movie *Grease*

- 1¼ ounces water

- 8¼ ounces Simple Syrup (page 18)

- 9 ounces lime juice

- 9 ounces Ceres peach juice

- **6¼ ounces Boulevard Tank 7 Farmhouse Ale**

- **6¼ ounces Pinckney Bend Gin**

Combine → Place the ingredients in a medium-size metal bowl and stir.

Freeze → Pour the liquid into a large freezer bag and place it in the freezer until frozen, approximately 4 hours. Alternatively, pour the liquid into an ice cream maker and proceed per the manufacturer's instructions (see page 11).

Serve → When you're ready to drink, massage the freezer bag by hand until it's a wet, slushy consistency. If it's not breaking up, run the bag quickly under hot water and massage some more.

Yield → Makes at least 4 drinks.

FRENCH AMERICAN

Stroll down the boulevards of Paris with the citrusy, cognac kick of this drink, and a splash of rosé finishing up on your palate.

ABV
10.45%

GLASS
Up & Down

GARNISH
lemon wheel, fleur-de-lis stencil (see page 23)

fleur-de-lis stencil

- 2¾ ounces water
- 8¼ ounces Simple Syrup (page 18)
- 8¼ ounces lemon juice
- **13¾ ounces rosé wine**
- **7 ounces Courvoisier Cognac**

Combine → Place the ingredients in a medium-size metal bowl and stir.

Freeze → Pour the liquid into a large freezer bag and place it in the freezer until frozen, approximately 4 hours. Alternatively, pour the liquid into an ice cream maker and proceed per the manufacturer's instructions (see page 11).

Serve → When you're ready to drink, massage the freezer bag by hand until it's a wet, slushy consistency. If it's not breaking up, run the bag quickly under hot water and massage some more.

Yield → Makes at least 4 drinks.

FETCH

A gentle freeze is just the kind of cool you need for a strawberry basil shrub with chardonnay and St-Germain elderflower liqueur. And we will not stop trying to make "fetch" happen, Gretchen.

ABV
7.38%

GLASS
Wendy Winer

GARNISH
strawberry on a skewer, with *Mean Girls*

- 12¼ ounces water

- 3¼ ounces Simple Syrup (page 18)

- 6 ounces Salt & Flint Strawberry Basil Shrub

- **12½ ounces Toasted Head Chardonnay**

- **6 ounces St-Germain Elderflower Liqueur**

Combine → Place the ingredients in a medium-size metal bowl and stir.

Freeze → Pour the liquid into a large freezer bag and place it in the freezer until frozen, approximately 4 hours. Alternatively, pour the liquid into an ice cream maker and proceed per the manufacturer's instructions (see page 11).

Serve → When you're ready to drink, massage the freezer bag by hand until it's a wet, slushy consistency. If it's not breaking up, run the bag quickly under hot water and massage some more.

Yield → Makes at least 4 drinks.

'MERICA

Celebrate the Fourth—or any day—proudly with this bourbon-laced, apple pie–inspired, flag-waving companion. Rosemary from the syrup adds a bit of an herbal kick to the finish.

ABV
12.56%

GLASS
Up & Down

GARNISH
American flag drink stirrer

- 2¾ ounces Rosemary Simple Syrup (page 19)
- 26¾ ounces apple cider
- **8 ounces Bulleit Bourbon Frontier Whiskey**
- **3¾ ounces Laird's Applejack**

Combine → Place the ingredients in a medium-size metal bowl and stir.

Freeze → Pour the liquid into a large freezer bag and place it in the freezer until frozen, approximately 4 hours. Alternatively, pour the liquid into an ice cream maker and proceed per the manufacturer's instructions (see page 11).

Serve → When you're ready to drink, massage the freezer bag by hand until it's a wet, slushy consistency. If it's not breaking up, run the bag quickly under hot water and massage some more.

Yield → Makes at least 4 drinks.

PISCO POSH

The classic Pisco Sour brought below freezing. A simple and refined use of pisco, lemon, and bitters.

ABV
9.82%

GLASS
Flared

GARNISH
lemon twist

- 15 ounces water
- 8 ounces Simple Syrup (page 18)
- 8 ounces lemon juice
- 9¼ ounces Pisco Portón
- ¼ ounce Angostura Bitters

Combine → Place the ingredients in a medium-size metal bowl and stir.

Freeze → Pour the liquid into a large freezer bag and place it in the freezer until frozen, approximately 4 hours. Alternatively, pour the liquid into an ice cream maker and proceed per the manufacturer's instructions (see page 11).

Serve → When you're ready to drink, massage the freezer bag by hand until it's a wet, slushy consistency. If it's not breaking up, run the bag quickly under hot water and massage some more.

Yield → Makes at least 4 drinks.

OH MY DARLIN'

Clementine and prosecco combine for a bright summer explosion. Be sure to use Real Grenadine to get the full effect, otherwise the true essence of this drink may be lost and gone forever.

ABV
3.74%

GLASS
Bubbles Bubbles

GARNISH
candied lemon wheel, orange luster dust

- 1½ ounces water
- 6¼ ounces Simple Syrup (page 18)
- 3¾ ounces lemon juice
- 5½ ounces lime juice
- 9¼ ounces Izze Sparkling Clementine soda
- 1½ ounces Liber & Co. Real Grenadine
- **3¼ ounces Dolin Dry Vermouth de Chambéry**
- **9¼ ounces La Marca Prosecco**

Combine → Place the ingredients in a medium-size metal bowl and stir.

Freeze → Pour the liquid into a large freezer bag and place it in the freezer until frozen, approximately 4 hours. Alternatively, pour the liquid into an ice cream maker and proceed per the manufacturer's instructions (see page 11).

Serve → When you're ready to drink, massage the freezer bag by hand until it's a wet, slushy consistency. If it's not breaking up, run the bag quickly under hot water and massage some more.

Yield → Makes at least 4 drinks.

WALKING DEAD

Our take on the classic zombie, and the only biter that Daryl Dixon might not shoot directly on sight.

ABV
12.04%

GLASS
Floral Bowl

GARNISH
blood orange slice

- 15¾ ounces water
- 4½ ounces Simple Syrup (page 18)
- 7¼ ounces lemon juice
- **4¼ ounces Beefeater London Dry Gin**
- **4¼ ounces Cointreau Triple Sec**
- **4¼ ounces Lillet Blanc**
- **Absinthe wash for each glass**

Combine → Place the water, simple syrup, lemon juice, gin, triple sec, and Lillet in a medium-size metal bowl and stir.

Freeze → Pour the liquid into a large freezer bag and place it in the freezer until frozen, approximately 4 hours. Alternatively, pour the liquid into an ice cream maker and proceed per the manufacturer's instructions (see page 11).

Serve → When you're ready to drink, massage the freezer bag by hand until it's a wet, slushy consistency. If it's not breaking up, run the bag quickly under hot water and massage some more. Pour a splash of absinthe in each serving glass and turn the glass to coat before adding the sloshie.

Yield → Makes at least 4 drinks.

RASPBERRY CORVETTE

A little twang from the apple cider vinegar merges with the tarragon simple syrup and black raspberry and elderflower flavors for a fast ride to happy town.

ABV
7.15%

GLASS
Floral Bowl

GARNISH
fresh raspberries

- 21½ ounces water
- 7¾ ounces Tarragon Simple Syrup (page 19)
- 1¼ ounces apple cider vinegar
- **4¾ ounces Tito's Handmade Vodka**
- **1½ ounces Chambord Liqueur**
- **3¾ ounces St-Germain Elderflower Liqueur**

Combine → Place the ingredients in a medium-size metal bowl and stir.

Freeze → Pour the liquid into a large freezer bag and place it in the freezer until frozen, approximately 4 hours. Alternatively, pour the liquid into an ice cream maker and proceed per the manufacturer's instructions (see page 11).

Serve → When you're ready to drink, massage the freezer bag by hand until it's a wet, slushy consistency. If it's not breaking up, run the bag quickly under hot water and massage some more.

Yield → Makes at least 4 drinks.

LEMON IN PARADISE

A simple—yet fresh—frozen orangeade and lemonade hybrid to make you feel like a kid again.

ABV
0%

GLASS
Round & Round

GARNISH
candied lemon and orange wheels

- 3½ ounces water
- 10¾ ounces Simple Syrup (page 18)
- 10¾ ounces lemon juice
- 5 ounces orange juice
- 10 ounces whole milk

Combine → Place the water, simple syrup, lemon juice, and orange juice in a medium-size metal bowl and stir.

Blend → Add the milk to the bowl slowly, using an immersion blender to emulsify the mixture.

Freeze → Pour the liquid into a large freezer bag and place it in the freezer until frozen, approximately 4 hours. Alternatively, pour the liquid into an ice cream maker and proceed per the manufacturer's instructions (see page 11).

Serve → When you're ready to drink, massage the freezer bag by hand until it's a wet, slushy consistency. If it's not breaking up, run the bag quickly under hot water and massage some more.

Yield → Makes at least 4 drinks.

SPICED

dapper dan
(page 96)

high on the hog
(page 126)

posh spice
(page 112)

the catcher in
the rye
(page 100)

DAPPER DAN

You won't have any constant sorrow once you get this frozen apple pie à la mode on your taste buds.

ABV
7.72%

GLASS
Coffreeze & Teas

GARNISH
crisp apple slices dipped in gold sugar

- 16¾ ounces Cider Boys First Press Apple Cider
- 5 ounces Stirrings Apple Liqueur
- 3¾ ounces Cinnamon-Infused Tito's Vodka (**page 20**)
- 14½ ounces whole milk

Combine → Place the apple cider, apple liqueur, and vodka in a medium-size metal bowl and stir.

Blend → Add the milk to the bowl slowly, using an immersion blender to emulsify the mixture.

Freeze → Pour the liquid into a large freezer bag and place it in the freezer until frozen, approximately 4 hours. Alternatively, pour the liquid into an ice cream maker and proceed per the manufacturer's instructions (see page 11).

Serve → When you're ready to drink, massage the freezer bag by hand until it's a wet, slushy consistency. If it's not breaking up, run the bag quickly under hot water and massage some more.

Yield → Makes at least 4 drinks.

TU CHAI

Are you feeling a bit stressed lately? Modern medicine falling short of your complaint? Then hush, hush, as the Tazo chai and the vanilla and orange notes of Tuaca make you forget all your worries.

ABV
7%

GLASS
Coffreeze & Teas

GARNISH
grated nutmeg

- 5¾ ounces Simple Syrup (page 18)
- **8 ounces Tuaca Liqueur**
- 6½ ounces whole milk
- 19¾ ounces Tazo Chai Tea Latte Concentrate

Combine → Place the simple syrup and Tuaca liqueur in a medium-size metal bowl and stir.

Blend → Combine the milk and the latte concentrate and add them to the bowl slowly, using an immersion blender to emulsify the mixture.

Freeze → Pour the liquid into a large freezer bag and place it in the freezer until frozen, approximately 4 hours. Alternatively, pour the liquid into an ice cream maker and proceed per the manufacturer's instructions (see page 11).

Serve → When you're ready to drink, massage the freezer bag by hand until it's a wet, slushy consistency. If it's not breaking up, run the bag quickly under hot water and massage some more.

Yield → Makes at least 4 drinks.

KOOKIE MONZTER

C is for cookie and it's good enough for . . . two, if you can bring yourself to share! It reallllly does taste like an oatmeal cookie, we swear.

ABV
9.03%

GLASS
Rippled

GARNISH
stencil with circles of varying sizes (see page 23)

circles stencil

- 11¼ ounces Simple Syrup (page 18)
- **3¼ ounces Boulaine Butterscotch Schnapps**
- **3¼ ounces Jägermeister**
- **3¼ ounces Goldschläger Cinnamon Schnapps**
- 15½ ounces whole milk
- **3¼ ounces Baileys Irish Cream**

Combine → Place the simple syrup, butterscotch schnapps, Jägermeister, and Goldschläger in a medium-size metal bowl and stir.

Blend → Combine the milk and the Baileys, and add them to the bowl slowly, using an immersion blender to emulsify the mixture.

Freeze → Pour the liquid into a large freezer bag and place it in the freezer until frozen, approximately 4 hours. Alternatively, pour the liquid into an ice cream maker and proceed per the manufacturer's instructions (see page 11).

Serve → When you're ready to drink, massage the freezer bag by hand until it's a wet, slushy consistency. If it's not breaking up, run the bag quickly under hot water and massage some more.

Yield → Makes at least 4 drinks.

WINTER IS COMING

Dubonnet Rouge (a fortified wine with herb and spice notes) and Hennessey duke it out for control of the throne, as absinthe lurks in the background, waiting to take its rightful place.

ABV
12.22%

GLASS
Floral Bowl

GARNISH
snowflake or direwolf stencil (see page 23)

direwolf stencil

- 17 ounces water
- 8½ ounces Simple Syrup (page 18)
- **4¼ ounces Dubonnet Rouge Aperitif Wine**
- **10¼ ounces Hennessy Cognac**
- **¼ teaspoon Angostura Bitters**
- **Absinthe wash for each glass**

Combine → Place the water, simple syrup, Dubonnet Rouge, Hennessy, and bitters in a medium-size metal bowl and stir.

Freeze → Pour the liquid into a large freezer bag and place it in the freezer until frozen, approximately 4 hours. Alternatively, pour the liquid into an ice cream maker and proceed per the manufacturer's instructions (see page 11).

Serve → When you're ready to drink, massage the freezer bag by hand until it's a wet, slushy consistency. If it's not breaking up, run the bag quickly under hot water and massage some more. Pour a splash of absinthe in each serving glass and turn the glass to coat before adding the sloshie.

Yield → Makes at least 4 drinks.

THE CATCHER IN THE RYE

Don your houndstooth coat and relive your teenage angst as you mix up this frozen version of an old-fashioned.

ABV
8.46%

GLASS
Up & Down

GARNISH
houndstooth stencil (see page 23) with infused cherry and orange wheel

- 10 ounces Simple Syrup (page 18)
- 5 ounces lemon juice
- 15¾ ounces orange juice
- **8¼ ounces Cherry-Infused Old Overholt Rye Whiskey** (page 21)

houndstooth stencil

Combine → Place the ingredients in a medium-size metal bowl and stir.

Freeze → Pour the liquid into a large freezer bag and place it in the freezer until frozen, approximately 4 hours. Alternatively, pour the liquid into an ice cream maker and proceed per the manufacturer's instructions (see page 11).

Serve → When you're ready to drink, massage the freezer bag by hand until it's a wet, slushy consistency. If it's not breaking up, run the bag quickly under hot water and massage some more.

Yield → Makes at least 4 drinks.

THE ROCKEFELLER

NYC's most famous ice—a perfectly balanced frozen Manhattan with rye-infused fresh cherries. Another top seller at Snow & Co.

ABV
9.74%

GLASS
Up & Down

GARNISH
cherries from infusion on skewer, black top-hat stencil (see page 23)

top-hat stencil

- 20 ounces water
- 8¼ ounces Simple Syrup (page 18)
- **3½ ounces Cinzano Rosso Sweet Vermouth**
- **8½ ounces Cherry-Infused Old Overholt Rye Whiskey (page 21)**
- **¼ teaspoon Angostura Bitters**

Combine → Place the ingredients in a medium-size metal bowl and stir.

Freeze → Pour the liquid into a large freezer bag and place it in the freezer until frozen, approximately 4 hours. Alternatively, pour the liquid into an ice cream maker and proceed per the manufacturer's instructions (see page 11).

Serve → When you're ready to drink, massage the freezer bag by hand until it's a wet, slushy consistency. If it's not breaking up, run the bag quickly under hot water and massage some more.

Yield → Makes at least 4 drinks.

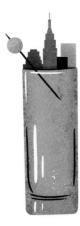

SPICED WINTER SHANDY

Even though this drink's consistency is reminiscent of any blizzard conditions that might be outside, the nutmeg and apple from the Catdaddy moonshine will warm your belly.

ABV
8.26%

GLASS
Up & Down

GARNISH
orange wheel

- 7½ ounces Simple Syrup (page 18)

- 10 ounces orange juice

- **17½ ounces Samuel Adams Winter Lager Beer**

- **1¾ ounces Catdaddy Spiced Moonshine**

- **3¼ ounces Junior Johnson Midnight Moon Apple Pie Moonshine**

Combine → Place the ingredients in a medium-size metal bowl and stir.

Freeze → Pour the liquid into a large freezer bag and place it in the freezer until frozen, approximately 4 hours. Alternatively, pour the liquid into an ice cream maker and proceed per the manufacturer's instructions (see page 11).

Serve → When you're ready to drink, massage the freezer bag by hand until it's a wet, slushy consistency. If it's not breaking up, run the bag quickly under hot water and massage some more.

Yield → Makes at least 4 drinks.

NOGGIN 'N' NICE

He knows if you've been bad or good, but he'll forget about your status on the naughty list if you put one of these by the chimney. Creamy smooth from the Tres Leches (triple-cream!) liqueur, with a heavy grating of nutmeg from the Catdaddy moonshine.

ABV
10.2%

GLASS
Coffreeze & Teas

GARNISH
grated nutmeg

- **4 ounces Crème de Cacao**
- **6 ounces Catdaddy Spiced Moonshine**
- **4 ounces Tres Leches Triple Cream Liqueur**
- 26 ounces whole milk

Combine → Place the crème de cacao, moonshine, and Tres Leches liqueur in a medium-size metal bowl and stir.

Blend → Add the milk to the bowl slowly, using an immersion blender to emulsify the mixture.

Freeze → Pour the liquid into a large freezer bag and place it in the freezer until frozen, approximately 4 hours. Alternatively, pour the liquid into an ice cream maker and proceed per the manufacturer's instructions (see page 11).

Serve → When you're ready to drink, massage the freezer bag by hand until it's a wet, slushy consistency. If it's not breaking up, run the bag quickly under hot water and massage some more.

Yield → Makes at least 4 drinks.

SUZE Q

Notes of gentian root in the Suze aperitif play with the orange and lemon citrus. Take it easy with this one so you don't end up blanc-ing out!

ABV
10.3%

GLASS
Floral Bowl

GARNISH
lemon twist, purple luster dust, exclamation point stencil (see page 23)

- 3 ounces water
- 9¼ ounces Simple Syrup (page 18)
- 9¼ ounces lemon juice
- 6¾ ounces orange juice
- 5½ ounces Lillet Blanc
- 3¼ ounces Cointreau Triple Sec
- 3¼ ounces Suze Aperitif Liqueur

Combine → Place the ingredients in a medium-size metal bowl and stir.

Freeze → Pour the liquid into a large freezer bag and place it in the freezer until frozen, approximately 4 hours. Alternatively, pour the liquid into an ice cream maker and proceed per the manufacturer's instructions (see page 11).

Serve → When you're ready to drink, massage the freezer bag by hand until it's a wet, slushy consistency. If it's not breaking up, run the bag quickly under hot water and massage some more.

Yield → Makes at least 4 drinks.

exclamation point stencil

BUSTA FROZEN

Jump jump gingerly with some elderflower and tell 'em to pass the Courvoisier (and Cocchi Americano).

ABV
8.58%

GLASS
Floral Bowl

GARNISH
peeled fresh ginger, grated

- 22 ounces ginger ale
- 5½ ounces Jack Rudy Elderflower Tonic
- **6 ounces Courvoisier Cognac**
- **6 ounces Cocchi Americano Aperitif Wine**

Combine → Place the ingredients in a medium-size metal bowl and stir.

Freeze → Pour the liquid into a large freezer bag and place it in the freezer until frozen, approximately 4 hours. Alternatively, pour the liquid into an ice cream maker and proceed per the manufacturer's instructions (see page 11).

Serve → When you're ready to drink, massage the freezer bag by hand until it's a wet, slushy consistency. If it's not breaking up, run the bag quickly under hot water and massage some more.

Yield → Makes at least 4 drinks.

XROADS ICED TEA

Long Island Iced Tea done with Kansas City style: frozen and subbing out the cola for root beer.

ABV
8.64%

GLASS
Flared

GARNISH
white "X" stencil
(see page 23)

"x" stencil

- 1½ ounces water
- 4¼ ounces Simple Syrup (page 18)
- 4¼ ounces lemon juice
- 21¾ ounces Whole Foods 365 Root Beer
- **1¾ ounces Bacardi White Rum**
- **1¾ ounces Beefeater London Dry Gin**
- **1¾ ounces Tito's Handmade Vodka**
- **1¾ ounces Herradura Tequila**
- **1¾ ounces Grand Marnier**

Combine → Place the ingredients in a medium-size metal bowl and stir.

Freeze → Pour the liquid into a large freezer bag and place it in the freezer until frozen, approximately 4 hours. Alternatively, pour the liquid into an ice cream maker and proceed per the manufacturer's instructions (see page 11).

Serve → When you're ready to drink, massage the freezer bag by hand until it's a wet, slushy consistency. If it's not breaking up, run the bag quickly under hot water and massage some more.

Yield → Makes at least 4 drinks.

MOJITO NIXON

While hunting for the anti-Elvis, we ran across this Mojito Nixon drink. There are a lot of unexplained phenomena out there, but mint and lime in harmony with Bacardi rum? It works. 'Nuff said.

ABV
6.64%

GLASS
Rippled

GARNISH
mint sprig, and a Jello Biafra song (just one, don't over-garnish)

- 1¼ ounces water
- 13½ ounces Mint Simple Syrup (page 19)
- 10¾ ounces lime juice
- **⅛ teaspoon Angostura Bitters**
- **6¾ ounces Bacardi White Rum**
- 8¼ ounces whole milk

Combine → Place the water, simple syrup, lime juice, Angostura bitters, and rum in a medium-size metal bowl and stir.

Blend → Add the milk to the bowl slowly, using an immersion blender to emulsify the mixture.

Freeze → Pour the liquid into a large freezer bag and place it in the freezer until frozen, approximately 4 hours. Alternatively, pour the liquid into an ice cream maker and proceed per the manufacturer's instructions (see page 11).

Serve → When you're ready to drink, massage the freezer bag by hand until it's a wet, slushy consistency. If it's not breaking up, run the bag quickly under hot water and massage some more.

Yield → Makes at least 4 drinks.

PINK SLIPPER

You'll be the belle of the ball when you slip this into everyone's glass at your party. Grapefruit is the perfect match for vodka infused with hints of ginger.

ABV
8.94%

GLASS
Rippled

GARNISH
candied grapefruit peel

- 5½ ounces water
- 8 ounces Agave Syrup (page 18)
- 17¾ ounces grapefruit juice
- **9 ounces Ginger-Infused Tito's Vodka (page 20)**

Combine → Place the ingredients in a medium-size metal bowl and stir.

Freeze → Pour the liquid into a large freezer bag and place it in the freezer until frozen, approximately 4 hours. Alternatively, pour the liquid into an ice cream maker and proceed per the manufacturer's instructions (see page 11).

Serve → When you're ready to drink, massage the freezer bag by hand until it's a wet, slushy consistency. If it's not breaking up, run the bag quickly under hot water and massage some more.

Yield → Makes at least 4 drinks.

SWEET GINGER

A stepsister to the pink slipper . . .
An indulgent pop of Domaine de Canton plus a little milk gives this charming sibling a velvety, creamy texture and taste.

ABV
5.59%

GLASS
Floral

GARNISH
candied ginger

- 7¾ ounces Agave Syrup (page 18)

- 18 ounces grapefruit juice

- **2¼ ounces Tito's Handmade Vodka**

- **6¾ ounces Domaine de Canton Ginger Liqueur**

- 5½ ounces whole milk

Combine → Place the agave syrup, grapefruit juice, vodka, and Domaine de Canton in a medium-size metal bowl and stir.

Blend → Add the milk to the bowl slowly, using an immersion blender to emulsify the mixture.

Freeze → Pour the liquid into a large freezer bag and place it in the freezer until frozen, approximately 4 hours. Alternatively, pour the liquid into an ice cream maker and proceed per the manufacturer's instructions (see page 11).

Serve → When you're ready to drink, massage the freezer bag by hand until it's a wet, slushy consistency. If it's not breaking up, run the bag quickly under hot water and massage some more.

Yield → Makes at least 4 drinks.

FUEGO DE LECHE

Fire up the gang with this spiced frozen lemonade. Jalapeño-infused vodka kicks it off, while the milk cools your tongue back down for the next sip.

ABV
10.13%

GLASS
Rippled

GARNISH
jalapeño wheel from the vodka infusion

- 3 ounces water
- 8½ ounces Simple Syrup (page 18)
- 8½ ounces lemon juice
- **7½ ounces Jalapeño-Infused Tito's Vodka (page 20)**
- **3 ounces Tuaca Liqueur**
- 9½ ounces whole milk

Combine → Place the water, simple syrup, lemon juice, vodka, and Tuaca liqueur in a medium-size metal bowl and stir.

Blend → Add the milk to the bowl slowly, using an immersion blender to emulsify the mixture.

Freeze → Pour the liquid into a large freezer bag and place it in the freezer until frozen, approximately 4 hours. Alternatively, pour the liquid into an ice cream maker and proceed per the manufacturer's instructions (see page 11).

Serve → When you're ready to drink, massage the freezer bag by hand until it's a wet, slushy consistency. If it's not breaking up, run the bag quickly under hot water and massage some more.

Yield → Makes at least 4 drinks.

PROUD MARY

Think you can't freeze a Bloody Mary? Think again. Pop in a dash or two of Worcestershire sauce if you're feeling even more adventurous.

ABV
6.74%

GLASS
Round & Round

GARNISH
celery and olive

- 1¼ ounces water
- 4¼ ounces Simple Syrup (page 18)
- 4¼ ounces lemon juice
- 10 ounces tomato juice
- **6¾ ounces Jalapeño-Infused Tito's Vodka (page 20)**
- 13½ ounces whole milk

Combine → Place the water, simple syrup, lemon juice, tomato juice, and vodka in a medium-size metal bowl and stir.

Blend → Add the milk to the bowl slowly, using an immersion blender to emulsify the mixture.

Freeze → Pour the liquid into a large freezer bag and place it in the freezer until frozen, approximately 4 hours. Alternatively, pour the liquid into an ice cream maker and proceed per the manufacturer's instructions (see page 11).

Serve → When you're ready to drink, massage the freezer bag by hand until it's a wet, slushy consistency. If it's not breaking up, run the bag quickly under hot water and massage some more.

Yield → Makes at least 4 drinks.

POSH SPICE

Tell us what you want, what you really, really want! Wait, we know: a pop of jalapeño over juicy passion fruit, with a finish of smoky mescal? It'll make you zig-a-zig ah . . .

ABV
8.89%

GLASS
Floral

GARNISH
passion fruit cube and jalapeño from syrup infusion on a skewer

- 1½ ounces water
- 5¾ ounces Simple Syrup (page 18)
- 4½ ounces lemon juice
- 19¾ ounces Whole Foods Tropical Blend Italian Soda
- **3 ounces Jalapeño-Infused Tito's Handmade Vodka (page 20)**
- **6 ounces Del Maguey Crema de Mezcal**

Combine → Place the ingredients in a medium-size metal bowl and stir.

Freeze → Pour the liquid into a large freezer bag and place it in the freezer until frozen, approximately 4 hours. Alternatively, pour the liquid into an ice cream maker and proceed per the manufacturer's instructions (see page 11).

Serve → When you're ready to drink, massage the freezer bag by hand until it's a wet, slushy consistency. If it's not breaking up, run the bag quickly under hot water and massage some more.

Yield → Makes at least 4 drinks.

THE WINTERGREEN FAIRY

Absinthe visits the frozen lands of the Fey, with notes of orange and rhubarb from the Aperol, as well as anise from the Pernod, wafting over the citrusy lemon.

ABV
12.21%

GLASS
Floral Bowl

GARNISH
green fairy dust

- 14¼ ounces water
- 12 ounces Mint Simple Syrup (page 19)
- 4¼ ounces lemon juice
- **8¾ ounces Aperol Aperitif**
- **7¾ ounces Pernod Absinthe**

Combine → Place the ingredients in a medium-size metal bowl and stir.

Freeze → Pour the liquid into a large freezer bag and place it in the freezer until frozen, approximately 4 hours. Alternatively, pour the liquid into an ice cream maker and proceed per the manufacturer's instructions (see page 11).

Serve → When you're ready to drink, massage the freezer bag by hand until it's a wet, slushy consistency. If it's not breaking up, run the bag quickly under hot water and massage some more.

Yield → Makes at least 4 drinks.

PITH OF DESPAIR

For our Chicago hipster friends, we took this dare to use Malört. Sweet grapefruit and gin up front, with the wormwood taste of Malört on the back end. A study in contrast. To paraphrase John Locke, when you finish, you'll know wormwood and grapefruit are not the same thing.

ABV
20.85%

GLASS
Floral Bowl

GARNISH
sorrow and despair

- 11¾ ounces Simple Syrup (page 18)
- 7¾ ounces grapefruit juice
- **9¾ ounces Koval Gin**
- **10¾ ounces Jeppson's Malört**

Combine → Place the ingredients in a medium-size metal bowl and stir.

Freeze → Pour the liquid into a large freezer bag and place it in the freezer until frozen, approximately 4 hours. Alternatively, pour the liquid into an ice cream maker and proceed per the manufacturer's instructions (see page 11).

Serve → When you're ready to drink, massage the freezer bag by hand until it's a wet, slushy consistency. If it's not breaking up, run the bag quickly under hot water and massage some more.

Yield → Makes at least 4 drinks.

FROZONI

For fans of the classic, we bring you the Negroni in frozen form. A splash of orange hits you first, and the Campari and vermouth finish the experience. A dry treat for those who want to veer away from sweet.

ABV
7.13%

GLASS
Flared

GARNISH
orange slice with lemon twist

- 10½ ounces water
- 1¾ ounces Simple Syrup (page 18)
- 1¾ ounces lemon juice
- 16¼ ounces orange juice
- **3½ ounces Cinzano Rosso Sweet Vermouth**
- **3½ ounces Pinckney Bend Gin**
- **3½ ounces Campari**

Combine → Place the ingredients in a medium-size metal bowl and stir.

Freeze → Pour the liquid into a large freezer bag and place it in the freezer until frozen, approximately 4 hours. Alternatively, pour the liquid into an ice cream maker and proceed per the manufacturer's instructions (see page 11).

Serve → When you're ready to drink, massage the freezer bag by hand until it's a wet, slushy consistency. If it's not breaking up, run the bag quickly under hot water and massage some more.

Yield → Makes at least 4 drinks.

FEZZIWIG'S FROZEN SPIRIT

If Fezziwig could freeze his Christmas feast drink for the summer, we'd like to imagine it would taste like this. Zesty orange and cinnamon, followed by fine port wine and apple. It's enough to warm the heart of Scrooge himself.

ABV
6.19%

GLASS
Wendy Winer

GARNISH
cinnamon stick, orange twist

- 5 ounces Simple Syrup (page 18)
- 25 ounces Cider Boys First Press Apple Cider
- 2½ ounces Dow's Fine Ruby Porto
- 7½ ounces Spiced Red Wine Infusion (page 22)

Combine → Place the ingredients in a medium-size metal bowl and stir.

Freeze → Pour the liquid into a large freezer bag and place it in the freezer until frozen, approximately 4 hours. Alternatively, pour the liquid into an ice cream maker and proceed per the manufacturer's instructions (see page 11).

Serve → When you're ready to drink, massage the freezer bag by hand until it's a wet, slushy consistency. If it's not breaking up, run the bag quickly under hot water and massage some more.

Yield → Makes at least 4 drinks.

WINTER LOG

A cold chocolate treat with hints of herbal warmth, orange, and saffron notes. Beware, this is basically just dessert in a glass.

ABV
8.25%

GLASS
Coffreeze & Teas

GARNISH
orange twist, chocolate shavings

- 2¾ ounces Simple Syrup (page 18)
- **2¾ ounces Gran Gala Triple Orange Liqueur**
- **2¾ ounces Tanqueray London Dry Gin**
- **2¾ ounces Strega Liqueur**
- 24½ ounces whole milk
- 4½ ounces Torani Dark Chocolate Sauce

Combine → Place the simple syrup, orange liqueur, gin, and Strega liqueur in a medium-size metal bowl and stir.

Blend → Combine the milk and the chocolate sauce and add them to the bowl slowly, using an immersion blender to emulsify the mixture.

Freeze → Pour the liquid into a large freezer bag and place it in the freezer until frozen, approximately 4 hours. Alternatively, pour the liquid into an ice cream maker and proceed per the manufacturer's instructions (see page 11).

Serve → When you're ready to drink, massage the freezer bag by hand until it's a wet, slushy consistency. If it's not breaking up, run the bag quickly under hot water and massage some more.

Yield → Makes at least 4 drinks.

HEART OF DARKNESS

A bittersweet surrender to artichoke and rum will take you up the river of flavor, past the honey and lemon and into the taste of Cynar. Not for the faint of heart.

ABV
10.53%

GLASS
Rippled

GARNISH
artichoke heart

- 4½ ounces water
- 13¼ ounces Simple Syrup (page 18)
- 3¼ ounces Honey Syrup (page 18)
- 4½ ounces lemon juice
- **6¾ ounces Cynar Liqueur**
- **7¾ ounces Bacardi White Rum**

Combine → Place the ingredients in a medium-size metal bowl and stir.

Freeze → Pour the liquid into a large freezer bag and place it in the freezer until frozen, approximately 4 hours. Alternatively, pour the liquid into an ice cream maker and proceed per the manufacturer's instructions (see page 11).

Serve → When you're ready to drink, massage the freezer bag by hand until it's a wet, slushy consistency. If it's not breaking up, run the bag quickly under hot water and massage some more.

Yield → Makes at least 4 drinks.

FERNET ABOUT IT

Lemon and lime start things up, with the herbalness of the Fernet bringing up the rear. If you haven't tried Fernet before, find a good watering hole to take a nip of it before venturing into this one blind.

ABV
7.97%

GLASS
Floral Bowl

GARNISH
gold luster-dust fleur-de-lis stencil (see pages 23 and 86)

- 6 ounces water
- 17¾ ounces Simple Syrup (page 18)
- 4½ ounces lemon juice
- 3 ounces lime juice
- **3 ounces Appleton Estate Jamaica Rum**
- **6 ounces Fernet-Branca Liqueur**
- **¾ teaspoon Fee Brothers Lemon Bitters**

Combine → Place the ingredients in a medium-size metal bowl and stir.

Freeze → Pour the liquid into a large freezer bag and place it in the freezer until frozen, approximately 4 hours. Alternatively, pour the liquid into an ice cream maker and proceed per the manufacturer's instructions (see page 11).

Serve → When you're ready to drink, massage the freezer bag by hand until it's a wet, slushy consistency. If it's not breaking up, run the bag quickly under hot water and massage some more.

Yield → Makes at least 4 drinks.

CHAMO JUICE

You may think you're invisible after two or three of these. Apple and citrus at the front are hiding a sly juniper and chamomile kicker. (The *h* is silent.)

ABV
9.06%

GLASS
Floral Bowl

GARNISH
chamomile sprig

- ¾ ounces water
- 7¼ ounces Simple Syrup (page 18)
- 4½ ounces lime juice
- 7½ ounces pineapple juice
- **7½ ounces Chamomile-Infused Gin (page 22)**
- **12½ ounces Cider Boys First Press Apple Cider**

Combine → Place the ingredients in a medium-size metal bowl and stir.

Freeze → Pour the liquid into a large freezer bag and place it in the freezer until frozen, approximately 4 hours. Alternatively, pour the liquid into an ice cream maker and proceed per the manufacturer's instructions (see page 11).

Serve → When you're ready to drink, massage the freezer bag by hand until it's a wet, slushy consistency. If it's not breaking up, run the bag quickly under hot water and massage some more.

Yield → Makes at least 4 drinks.

CRIMSON TIDE

A drier cousin to the Rockefeller (see page 101). The citrus at the front gets washed over by the black currant, and Campari at the end adds some woodsy notes.

ABV
10.43%

GLASS
Up & Down

GARNISH
black currants

- 18¾ ounces water
- 4½ ounces Simple Syrup (page 18)
- 4½ ounces lemon juice
- **7½ ounces Old Overholt Rye Whiskey**
- **2½ ounces Campari**
- **2½ ounces Crème de Cassis**

Combine → Place the ingredients in a medium-size metal bowl and stir.

Freeze → Pour the liquid into a large freezer bag and place it in the freezer until frozen, approximately 4 hours. Alternatively, pour the liquid into an ice cream maker and proceed per the manufacturer's instructions (see page 11).

Serve → When you're ready to drink, massage the freezer bag by hand until it's a wet, slushy consistency. If it's not breaking up, run the bag quickly under hot water and massage some more.

Yield → Makes at least 4 drinks.

DALY'S NIGHTLY

Golfers rejoice! Here's a new way to keep that iced tea and lemonade boozy and cold on the links. Grab your thermos—it's the same as the classic Arnold Palmer you're used to, just boozy and perfectly frozen.

ABV
10%

GLASS
Coffreeze & Teas

GARNISH
gold golf club cocktail stirrer

- 2¾ ounces water
- 8¼ ounces Simple Syrup (page 18)
- 8¼ ounces lemon juice
- **10 ounces Firefly Sweet Tea Vodka**
- 10¾ ounces whole milk

Combine → Place the water, simple syrup, lemon juice, and vodka in a medium-size metal bowl and stir.

Blend → Add the milk to the bowl slowly, using an immersion blender to emulsify the mixture.

Freeze → Pour the liquid into a large freezer bag and place it in the freezer until frozen, approximately 4 hours. Alternatively, pour the liquid into an ice cream maker and proceed per the manufacturer's instructions (see page 11).

Serve → When you're ready to drink, massage the freezer bag by hand until it's a wet, slushy consistency. If it's not breaking up, run the bag quickly under hot water and massage some more.

Yield → Makes at least 4 drinks.

THE GINGER GRANT

Boozy but easy drinking, this drink will be the object of everyone's desire. Citrus from the lime will light you up, followed by a pop of ginger at the end.

ABV
8.42%

GLASS
Bubbles Bubbles

GARNISH
lime twist

- 1¼ ounces water

- 4 ounces Simple Syrup (page 18)

- 8 ounces lime juice

- 18¾ ounces Gosling's Ginger Beer

- **8 ounces Pinckney Bend Gin**

- **¼ ounce Fee Brothers Cranberry Bitters**

Combine → Place the ingredients in a medium-size metal bowl and stir.

Freeze → Pour the liquid into a large freezer bag and place it in the freezer until frozen, approximately 4 hours. Alternatively, pour the liquid into an ice cream maker and proceed per the manufacturer's instructions (see page 11).

Serve → When you're ready to drink, massage the freezer bag by hand until it's a wet, slushy consistency. If it's not breaking up, run the bag quickly under hot water and massage some more.

Yield → Makes at least 4 drinks.

CAFÉ AMERICAS

A pick-me-up for a hot summer afternoon (or morning, if this is how you choose to get your caffeine), this adult version of a frappé starts out with coffee, continues with amaretto washing over your palate . . . and then the fireball hits you.

ABV
8.66%

GLASS
Coffreeze & Teas

GARNISH
cinnamon stick

- 7¾ ounces water
- 3 ounces Simple Syrup (page 18)
- 18¼ ounces freshly brewed coffee
- **8 ounces Fireball Cinnamon Whisky**
- **3¼ ounces Trader Vic's Amaretto Liqueur**
- **1 teaspoon Fee Brothers Chocolate Bitters**

Combine → Place the ingredients in a medium-size metal bowl and stir.

Freeze → Pour the liquid into a large freezer bag and place it in the freezer until frozen, approximately 4 hours. Alternatively, pour the liquid into an ice cream maker and proceed per the manufacturer's instructions (see page 11).

Serve → When you're ready to drink, massage the freezer bag by hand until it's a wet, slushy consistency. If it's not breaking up, run the bag quickly under hot water and massage some more.

Yield → Makes at least 4 drinks.

DUKE OF EARL

Pinkies up! You'll feel like English royalty with this frozen and spirited take on teatime in the countryside.

ABV
8.47%

GLASS
Floral Bowl

GARNISH
lemon wheel

- 2 ounces water
- 6 ounces Simple Syrup (page 18)
- 4 ounces Honey Syrup (page 18)
- 6 ounces lemon juice
- 14 ounces Earl Grey tea (steeped)
- **8¼ ounces Hendrick's Gin**

Combine → Place the ingredients in a medium-size metal bowl and stir.

Freeze → Pour the liquid into a large freezer bag and place it in the freezer until frozen, approximately 4 hours. Alternatively, pour the liquid into an ice cream maker and proceed per the manufacturer's instructions (see page 11).

Serve → When you're ready to drink, massage the freezer bag by hand until it's a wet, slushy consistency. If it's not breaking up, run the bag quickly under hot water and massage some more.

Yield → Makes at least 4 drinks.

HIGH ON THE HOG

Bacon is the candy of meats. It's so delicious, we decided just to build a drink around it. Ginger, maple, and bourbon roll on your tongue while you fight the urge to just eat the bacon garnish first.

ABV
12.78%

GLASS
Up & Down

GARNISH
strip of crispy bacon

- 27 ounces ginger ale
- **2 ounces Dolin Dry Vermouth de Chambéry**
- **2¾ ounces Cabin Fever Maple Flavored Whisky**
- **8¼ ounces Buffalo Trace Kentucky Straight Bourbon Whiskey**

Combine → Place the ingredients in a medium-size metal bowl and stir.

Freeze → Pour the liquid into a large freezer bag and place it in the freezer until frozen, approximately 4 hours. Alternatively, pour the liquid into an ice cream maker and proceed per the manufacturer's instructions (see page 11).

Serve → When you're ready to drink, massage the freezer bag by hand until it's a wet, slushy consistency. If it's not breaking up, run the bag quickly under hot water and massage some more.

Yield → Makes at least 4 drinks.

GARNISH GAME

Although the basics of Frozen Flair are covered on page 23, here are a few more tips to bump up your sloshie aesthetic. A fancy flourish will signal to your guests that this frozen cocktail is not your run-of-the-mill margarita.

A good rule of thumb is to **add fresh to frozen**. Consider the following: springs of herbs—especially thyme, rosemary, and basil; the leaves on a pineapple top; edible flowers (these can be procured online or at your local farmers' market); or full slices of fruits, including orange, grapefruit, lemon, lime, peach, plum, apple, or pear. **Seek out dramatic (read: unusual) varieties** like dragonfruit, kiwi, star fruit, watermelon, blood orange, cantaloupe, and honeydew. If there's a substantial rind, cut a half-inch notch in the fruit close to the rind and wedge the cocktail glass into the notch so the fruit stands vertically. And **don't forget the vegetables** for the more savory drinks—load up that Proud Mary (right, and page 111) with celery stalks, olives, cornichons, grape tomatoes, shrimp, lemon wedges, avocado, cocktail onions, Italian parsley . . . almost anything goes for this veritable salad of a beverage.

FLORAL

john larroquette
sex dream #2
(page 131)

cloud 9
(page 132)

violette's exit
(page 133)

benny and de june
(page 139)

JOHN LARROQUETTE SEX DREAM #1

When Snow & Co. was desperate for Facebook fans, we made a deal with someone—if she helped us, we'd name a drink after her lurid fever dream featuring John Larroquette. The coffee represents Dan Fielding's work side from the TV show *Night Court*. The tequila his naughty side.

ABV
9.32%

GLASS
Coffreeze & Teas

GARNISH
coffee cup stencil
(see page 23)

- 3¼ ounces Simple Syrup (page 18)
- 18 ounces freshly brewed coffee, cooled to room temperature
- **6¼ ounces Fruit Lab Hibiscus Liqueur**
- **6¼ ounces Olmeca Altos Reposado Tequila**
- 7½ ounces whole milk

Combine → Place the simple syrup, coffee, hibiscus liqueur, and tequila in a medium-size metal bowl and stir.

Blend → Add the milk to the bowl slowly, using an immersion blender to emulsify the mixture.

Freeze → Pour the liquid into a large freezer bag and place it in the freezer until frozen, approximately 4 hours. Alternatively, pour the liquid into an ice cream maker and proceed per the manufacturer's instructions (see page 11).

Serve → When you're ready to drink, massage the freezer bag by hand until it's a wet, slushy consistency. If it's not breaking up, run the bag quickly under hot water and massage some more.

Yield → Makes at least 4 drinks.

JOHN LARROQUETTE SEX DREAM #2

How can you just have one dreamy dalliance with John Larroquette? Close to the original, but with Soho instead of hibiscus.

ABV
9.53%

GLASS
Coffreeze & Teas

GARNISH
white luster-dusted coffee cup stencil (see page 23)

coffee cup stencil

- 3 ¼ ounces Simple Syrup (page 18)
- 18 ounces freshly brewed coffee, cooled to room temperature
- **6 ¼ ounces Soho Lychee Liqueur**
- **6 ¼ ounces Olmeca Altos Reposado Tequila**
- 6 ¼ ounces whole milk

Combine → Place the simple syrup, coffee, lychee liqueur, and tequila in a medium-size metal bowl and stir.

Blend → Add the milk to the bowl slowly, using an immersion blender to emulsify the mixture.

Freeze → Pour the liquid into a large freezer bag and place it in the freezer until frozen, approximately 4 hours. Alternatively, pour the liquid into an ice cream maker and proceed per the manufacturer's instructions (see page 11).

Serve → When you're ready to drink, massage the freezer bag by hand until it's a wet, slushy consistency. If it's not breaking up, run the bag quickly under hot water and massage some more.

Yield → Makes at least 4 drinks.

CLOUD 9

Light and fluffy, like drinking a dream. Two elderflowers—Thatcher's balanced with St-Germain—bring just the right amount of floral to the drink, without the sweetness becoming overpowering. Rounded out on the end with peach liqueur.

ABV
4.73%

GLASS
Rippled

GARNISH
gold luster dust, elderflower blossom

- 7¼ ounces Simple Syrup (page 18)
- **4¾ ounces Stirrings Peach Liqueur**
- **3½ ounces Thatcher's Organic Elderflower Liqueur**
- **2½ ounces St-Germain Elderflower Liqueur**
- 21¾ ounces whole milk

Combine → Place the simple syrup, the peach liqueur, and the two elderflower liqueurs in a medium-size metal bowl and stir.

Blend → Add the milk to the bowl slowly, using an immersion blender to emulsify the mixture.

Freeze → Pour the liquid into a large freezer bag and place it in the freezer until frozen, approximately 4 hours. Alternatively, pour the liquid into an ice cream maker and proceed per the manufacturer's instructions (see page 11).

Serve → When you're ready to drink, massage the freezer bag by hand until it's a wet, slushy consistency. If it's not breaking up, run the bag quickly under hot water and massage some more.

Yield → Makes at least 4 drinks.

VIOLETTE'S EXIT

Hendrick's is gin.
Violets are blue.
This drink is tasty,
*   and refreshing, too.*
Zesty with lemon . . .
We forgot our rhyme.
(This drink is strong.)

ABV
11.95%

GLASS
Floral Bowl

GARNISH
purple luster dust,
violet petals

- 18¾ ounces SanPellegrino Sparkling Lemon Beverage
- **3¼ ounces Rothman & Winter Crème de Violette**
- **10 ounces Hendrick's Gin**
- 8 ounces whole milk

Combine → Place the lemon SanPellegrino, crème de violette, and gin in a medium-size metal bowl and stir.

Blend → Add the milk to the bowl slowly, using an immersion blender to emulsify the mixture.

Freeze → Pour the liquid into a large freezer bag and place it in the freezer until frozen, approximately 4 hours. Alternatively, pour the liquid into an ice cream maker and proceed per the manufacturer's instructions (see page 11).

Serve → When you're ready to drink, massage the freezer bag by hand until it's a wet, slushy consistency. If it's not breaking up, run the bag quickly under hot water and massage some more.

Yield → Makes at least 4 drinks.

MIDNIGHT ORCHARD

This nocturnal concoction is like a good record that you just can't wrap your head around the first time. Give it a couple of spins to let the true musical genius settle in. Citrus and maraschino followed by whiskey and elderflower notes.

ABV
10.34%

GLASS
Floral Bowl

GARNISH
honeycomb, elderflower blossom

- 18¼ ounces water
- 7 ounces Honey Syrup (page 18)
- 2½ ounces lemon juice
- 5¾ ounces J. Rieger & Co. Whiskey
- 2 ounces Luxardo Maraschino Liqueur
- 4¼ ounces St-Germain Elderflower Liqueur
- ¼ ounce Fee Brothers Gin Barrel–Aged Orange Bitters

Combine → Place the ingredients in a medium-size metal bowl and stir.

Freeze → Pour the liquid into a large freezer bag and place it in the freezer until frozen, approximately 4 hours. Alternatively, pour the liquid into an ice cream maker and proceed per the manufacturer's instructions (see page 11).

Serve → When you're ready to drink, massage the freezer bag by hand until it's a wet, slushy consistency. If it's not breaking up, run the bag quickly under hot water and massage some more.

Yield → Makes at least 4 drinks.

SPARROW'S SWAGGER

It smells like treasure on the beach. It might even expand your vocabulary, or change your accent. This falernum (tasting of almond, ginger, cloves, and lime) and rum elixir combines rich castaways and Caribbean dreams. Try to stay out of trouble when drinking this one, you dirty pirate, you.

ABV
10.73%

GLASS
Flared

GARNISH
lime wheel

- 2 ounces water
- 8 ounces Simple Syrup (page 18)
- 16¼ ounces lime juice
- **9 ounces Cruzan 9 Spiced Rum**
- **4½ ounces John D. Taylor's Velvet Falernum Liqueur**
- **¼ ounce teaspoon Bitter Truth Golden Falernum Spiced Rum Liqueur**

Combine → Place the ingredients in a medium-size metal bowl and stir.

Freeze → Pour the liquid into a large freezer bag and place it in the freezer until frozen, approximately 4 hours. Alternatively, pour the liquid into an ice cream maker and proceed per the manufacturer's instructions (see page 11).

Serve → When you're ready to drink, massage the freezer bag by hand until it's a wet, slushy consistency. If it's not breaking up, run the bag quickly under hot water and massage some more.

Yield → Makes at least 4 drinks.

EAU DE GOLDEN GIRLS

Blanche sprays this on to drive the suitors wild. It's also a great frozen cocktail. Rose and herbal notes round out the front end of lemon. The vodka is there because . . . well, isn't that what Blanche would want?

ABV
8.57%

GLASS
Floral Bowl

GARNISH
rose petals, rose stencil
(see page 23)

- 4 ounces water
- 12½ ounces Simple Syrup (page 18)
- 12½ ounces lemon juice
- **3¾ ounces Tito's Handmade Vodka**
- **3¾ ounces Combier Liqueur de Rose**
- **3¾ ounces Amaro Nonino Quintessentia**

rose stencil

Combine → Place the ingredients in a medium-size metal bowl and stir.

Freeze → Pour the liquid into a large freezer bag and place it in the freezer until frozen, approximately 4 hours. Alternatively, pour the liquid into an ice cream maker and proceed per the manufacturer's instructions (see page 11).

Serve → When you're ready to drink, massage the freezer bag by hand until it's a wet, slushy consistency. If it's not breaking up, run the bag quickly under hot water and massage some more.

Yield → Makes at least 4 drinks.

GANDALF'S STAFF

You shall not pass (up) this IPA-inspired frozen shandy. Elderflower always plays nicely with twisted grapefruit and the hoppiness is a gift from our Ent friends. If you're looking to work some masterful frozen cocktail wizardry or bring down an evil empire of heat, here's your weapon of choice. New Belgium Ranger IPA is a good sub for the Boulevard here.

ABV
3.9%

GLASS
Pils & Chills

GARNISH
grapefruit twist

- ¾ ounce water
- 1¾ ounces Simple Syrup (page 18)
- 1¾ ounces lemon juice
- 11¼ ounces grapefruit juice
- **1¾ ounces Thatcher's Organic Elderflower Liqueur**
- **22¾ ounces Boulevard Single-Wide IPA**

Combine → Place the ingredients in a medium-size metal bowl and stir.

Freeze → Pour the liquid into a large freezer bag and place it in the freezer until frozen, approximately 4 hours. Alternatively, pour the liquid into an ice cream maker and proceed per the manufacturer's instructions (see page 11).

Serve → When you're ready to drink, massage the freezer bag by hand until it's a wet, slushy consistency. If it's not breaking up, run the bag quickly under hot water and massage some more.

Yield → Makes at least 4 drinks.

BEEZ KNEEZ

Sweet yet floral, this mix of apricot, chrysanthemum, and honey will have you buzzing from place to place, stopping to smell the flowers on your journey.

ABV
6.15%

GLASS
Floral Bowl

GARNISH
edible flower

- 7¼ ounces Simple Syrup (page 18)
- **4¾ ounces Rothman & Winter Orchard Apricot Liqueur**
- **6¾ ounces Koval Chrysanthemum and Honey Liqueur**
- 21¾ ounces whole milk

Combine → Place the simple syrup, apricot liqueur, and chrysanthemum and honey liqueur in a medium-size metal bowl and stir.

Blend → Add the milk to the bowl slowly, using an immersion blender to emulsify the mixture.

Freeze → Pour the liquid into a large freezer bag and place it in the freezer until frozen, approximately 4 hours. Alternatively, pour the liquid into an ice cream maker and proceed per the manufacturer's instructions (see page 11).

Serve → When you're ready to drink, massage the freezer bag by hand until it's a wet, slushy consistency. If it's not breaking up, run the bag quickly under hot water and massage some more.

Yield → Makes at least 4 drinks.

BENNY AND DE JUNE

A perfect pairing of two kindred spirits. The nose of the drink is decidedly juniper, while the flavor is a delicate melding of the one-of-a-kind Esprit de June vine flower liqueur—yes, that's a spirit made from the tiny white flowers of grapevines—and woodland pine notes from the gin.

ABV
9.34%

GLASS
Flared

GARNISH
juniper berries

- 9½ ounces water
- 10¼ ounces Simple Syrup (page 18)
- 10¼ ounces lemon juice
- **5 ounces Koval Gin**
- **5 ounces Esprit de June Liqueur**
- **1 teaspoon Angostura Bitters**

Combine → Place the ingredients in a medium-size metal bowl and stir.

Freeze → Pour the liquid into a large freezer bag and place it in the freezer until frozen, approximately 4 hours. Alternatively, pour the liquid into an ice cream maker and proceed per the manufacturer's instructions (see page 11).

Serve → When you're ready to drink, massage the freezer bag by hand until it's a wet, slushy consistency. If it's not breaking up, run the bag quickly under hot water and massage some more.

Yield → Makes at least 4 drinks.

NETFLIX AND CHILL

No alcoholic hanky-panky here. Now you can really just watch Netflix and literally chill. A refreshing cucumber and lime front finishes up with mint as it helps you wash down another episode of that original series you've been binging on.

ABV
0%

GLASS
Round & Round

GARNISH
a Netflix account

- 1¼ ounces water
- 7¾ ounces Mint Simple Syrup (page 19)
- 9 ounces lime juice
- 22¼ ounces DRY Sparkling Cucumber soda

Combine → Place the ingredients in a medium-size metal bowl and stir.

Freeze → Pour the liquid into a large freezer bag and place it in the freezer until frozen, approximately 4 hours. Alternatively, pour the liquid into an ice cream maker and proceed per the manufacturer's instructions (see page 11).

Serve → When you're ready to drink, massage the freezer bag by hand until it's a wet, slushy consistency. If it's not breaking up, run the bag quickly under hot water and massage some more.

Yield → Makes at least 4 drinks.

SEA-BISCUS

We're off to the races with another alcohol-free frozen delicacy! Tart, tropical hibiscus is a nice flavor follow-up to the juicy blend of pomegranate and tangerine.

ABV
0%

GLASS
Coffreeze & Teas

GARNISH
tangerine wheel

- 21 ounces hibiscus tea (steeped)

- 9¼ ounces Simple Syrup (page 18)

- 9¼ ounces Whole Foods Tangerine Italian soda

- ¾ ounce Liber & Co. Grenadine

Combine → Place the ingredients in a medium-size metal bowl and stir.

Freeze → Pour the liquid into a large freezer bag and place it in the freezer until frozen, approximately 4 hours. Alternatively, pour the liquid into an ice cream maker and proceed per the manufacturer's instructions (see page 11).

Serve → When you're ready to drink, massage the freezer bag by hand until it's a wet, slushy consistency. If it's not breaking up, run the bag quickly under hot water and massage some more.

Yield → Makes at least 4 drinks.

BLUE MONDAY

After hitting the sauce over the weekend, give your body some time off with a hit of ice cold antioxidants.

ABV
0%

GLASS
Rippled

GARNISH
fresh blueberries

- 1¼ ounces water
- 4¼ ounces Simple Syrup (page 18)
- 10 ounces lime juice
- 8 ounces Lemon SanPellegrino
- 16½ ounces R.W. Knudsen Just Blueberry Juice

Combine → Place the ingredients in a medium-size metal bowl and stir.

Freeze → Pour the liquid into a large freezer bag and place it in the freezer until frozen, approximately 4 hours. Alternatively, pour the liquid into an ice cream maker and proceed per the manufacturer's instructions (see page 11).

Serve → When you're ready to drink, massage the freezer bag by hand until it's a wet, slushy consistency. If it's not breaking up, run the bag quickly under hot water and massage some more.

Yield → Makes at least 4 drinks.

APPENDIX #1
MIX IT UP

The coolest thing we ever learned was that mixing these cocktails together would bring great (and sometimes unexpected) flavors. Here are a few of our favorites for you to try.

THE PURPLE BASTARD

Limey Bastard (gin, lime, and cucumber base) **+ Purple Rain** (Chambord and blueberry base)

Starts with the raspberry and blueberry, then a lingering taste of lime and some cucumber on the finish.

THE JUICY PEAR

The O'Connell (Jameson and citrus base) **+ The Elphaba** (Midori and peach base)

We swear it tastes like a juicy pear. Not an artificial pear. An honest to goodness glass of (boozy) pear juiciness.

KEY LIME

Cloud 9 (elderflower and peach base) **+ Limey Bastard** (gin, lime, and cucumber base)

Lime up front with the elderflower and peach following up at the end.

WITCHY WOMAN

Miss Scarlett (bourbon and lemon base) **+ The Elphaba** (Midori and peach base)

Tart lemon and bourbon with a kiss of sweetness and melon at the end.

MS. CLAUS TIPPLER

Noggin 'n' Nice (chocolate and spiced moonshine base) **+ The Rockefeller** (cherry rye base)

Like a spicy cherry chocolate shake.

THE CHAD

Named after the first person to mix all available flavors at Snow & Co. You can name it after the first person to do so at your party. It's like a tasting at Willy Wonka's factory. Make sure you have five to ten flavors to mix before allowing an attempt.

DO THE WALRUS

Want to mix flavors like a pro? Then do like we do at Snow & Co.: Grab two straws and pick the flavors you'd like to mix. Now look in a mirror. See the resemblance?

APPENDIX #2
FLIGHTS OF FROZEN

While you may be a convert after making all of our cocktails, you may encounter a friend or two who can be a bit hard to reach. The best way to bring them into the fold? Flights of frozen cocktails, my friend! Bodum makes a three-ounce glass that we use for flights at Snow & Co., but you can use any short glass to serve. Flights let you get a sense of the flavors and find your favorite without committing to a whole drink, which is what most people need to try something new.

Keep the sloshie mixtures in the freezer until right before serving. Double-walled glassware will keep them cold longer, but you've got about five minutes of optimal serving time for a flight due to the smaller size (we suggest three ounces of each cocktail). If you're serving a large group, you can get the product ready and in the flight glasses, then stick them back in the freezer. It will hold for about thirty minutes before they start to freeze solid in the glasses.

Shh—this may be blasphemy, but we're going to suggest fun over flavor here. Most flights are based on commonalities. We want you to explore, since we find people are often surprised by what they like when they stretch their boundaries. Here are a few suggestions for how to style your flights.

HOW TO POUR:

Don't have three or four machines on hand like we do at Snow & Co.? No worries! If you pour the sloshie mixtures into large freezer bags and cut the tip off you can pour shot-size sloshies just as if you were piping icing onto a cupcake.

OOPS! DID YOUR SLOSHIE GET SOUPY?

Throw it back in the freezer and it'll set back up in a few hours. Pro tip: If you have a large volume of the same drink that is still frozen, you can mix the soupy portion into it and it will set back up faster.

2 X 2

Pick two each from opposing categories (sweet and tart or spiced and floral) and take your guests on a roller-coaster ride of a tasting trip.

FOUR OF A KIND

Grab your four favorites from one category and place them out for friends. Color becomes more of a differentiator than anything here, as the flair of the color combinations and garnishes will make you the frozen rock star of your friends.

DANDY SHANDIES

Shandies are a great summertime treat, even more so when frozen. Grab our Sunshine Boulevard (page 38), Gose in the Shell (page 67), and Bulleit with IPA Wings (page 39), and pair them up to cool down a hot summer.

GINNED UP

Put on some flapper attire and throw these frozen gin favorites in line for tasting: Limey Bastard (page 41), Benny and de June (page 139), and the Frozoni (page 115).

CORNERS OF THE MAP

Pick one each from the sweet, tart, spiced, and floral chapters to test your taste buds.

BOURBON BUDDIES

Coming this season on FZN: One is a southern peach (Miss Scarlett, page 42), one is a city slickin' barista (Barista Life, page 83), and the other is hard-riding jockey (Whiskey Smashed, page 32). See what hilarity ensues when you get them in an apartment together!

BOBCAT GOLDTHWAIT'S COCKTAIL PARTY

You can't fit it into a category, but you'll never forget it for the rest of your life. Three unique frozen cocktails that hit you like a freight train and don't stop: Pith of Despair (page 114), Nights of Ni (page 46), and The Wintergreen Fairy (page 113).

THREE LITTLE FONZIES

What are Fonzies like, Yolanda? That's right, cool! Correctamundo. In fact, ice cold. Try this flight of our most unique cocktails: Benny and de June (page 139), Hemingway's Jazz (page 65), and Gose in the Shell (page 67).

APPENDIX #3
DRINKS, ALPHABETICALLY

APPENDIX #4
DRINKS, BY LIQUOR